LIGHT SPACE LIFE

HOUSES BY SAOTA

LIGHT SPACE LIFE

HOUSES BY SAOTA

With over 500 illustrations

T&H

CONTENTS

FOREWORD 06 by Reni Folawiyo

INTRODUCTION 08

10 OCEAN VIEW Cape Town South Africa

22 KLOOF HOUSE Cape Town South Africa

36 BEYOND Cape Town South Africa

48 BOMA Cape Town South Africa

60 KLOOF 145 Cape Town South Africa

72 CRESCENT Cape Town South Africa

THE SOUTH AFRICAN HOUSE 82 by Nic Coetzer

90 SILVER BAY Shelley Point South Africa

102 ULUWATU Bali Indonesia

116 BORA Mallorca Spain

128 RESTIO RIVER Pringle Bay South Africa

140 LA LUCIA Durban South Africa

152 BEACHY HEAD Plettenberg Bay South Africa

PATRONS 166 by Stefan Antoni

172 VENUS Cape Town South Africa

184 DI LIDO Miami USA

196 TERRACINA Miami USA

206 DOUBLE BAY Sydney Australia

218 SILVER PINE Moscow Russia

228 IKOYI Lagos Nigeria

COLLABORATION 244

250 LAKE HOUSE Lake Geneva Switzerland

260 COURBE Lac Leman Switzerland

274 HURON Ontario Canada

286 STRADELLA Los Angeles USA

298 HILLSIDE Los Angeles USA

TIMELINE 310

CREDITS 318

FOREWORD

Reni Folawiyo

As a great lover of all things art and design, and an unapologetic proponent of the brilliance of Africa and its contemporary language, I had followed the work of SAOTA for many years before meeting and being completely charmed by Stefan Antoni, and subsequently working with the SAOTA team on our homes. I was delighted to be asked to write the foreword to this book. It gives me a chance not only to give context to my admiration of SAOTA's work but to be part of this long-overdue book, a representation of thirty years' worth of dynamic, innovative, thoughtful masterpieces that capture the craft and essence of SAOTA. This book also shows how its language has travelled continents and captured the imagination of clients like me all around the world from Cape Town to Dakar, Lagos, Sydney, Los Angeles, Miami, Bali, Geneva and Mallorca.

This was always going to be an exciting relationship. An African architecture firm that had established a contemporary African language and a strong visual identity. A team that had broken barriers and was able to impose on the world a clear, strong message of its contemporary cutting-edge approach. And then myself, also an Africanist, with a world view and broad eclectic taste grounded in my vast knowledge of and interest in art and design, a focus of my work in ALÁRA as a curator and retailer guiding and representing what it is to live as Africans today. As professionals coming together on this personal project, we brought several genres to the design of our Lagos family home, Ikoyi (see page 228), and the breadth of these interests has combined to express a vision of contemporary African luxury and lifestyle.

This collaboration, in both its process and its execution, exceeded my already high expectations. Walking into our space you can tell you're in a SAOTA building. It's the way they expertly merge indoor and outdoor spaces with simple dramatic lines. It's the vast spaces that incorporate elements that are specifically suited to simple modern family living. But it's also the grand proportions that transform the home from family cocoon to a space that allows for my favourite dramatic accessories and our regular sprawling parties.

The building itself, with its tall imposing white branches and dramatic screens that frame our floating infinity pool, acts like a huge window that allows us intimate enjoyment of lush green treetops from the inside of the house – a rare find in built-up Lagos. This was another thoughtful, inclusive moment in the SAOTA architecture of the type that you will find in abundance in this book. At first glance, the building could be seen as almost an antithesis to the vernacular of the city, but not really: I see it almost as a direction of the future of our city and as the beginning of the language the city could have. Our city is throbbing in anticipation of its own greatness and I believe it's one that welcomes bold modernist architecture.

Adam Court and I had a lot of fun researching and collecting pieces for the interior, which we wanted to reflect my desire to have a contemporary African home. I wanted a space that was sophisticated yet unpolished, warm and artistic, where vastly different design pieces were layered together in a cohesive way that celebrated the beauty of each piece and the emotion of the art. In the end that was not hard at all to achieve. It was an instinctive, intuitive process led by my desire to be surrounded by meaningful, exquisite beauty and to have someone who understood that right beside me – how delightful!

For the interiors, we had a sprawling, voluminous, zen base that allowed us the luxury of travel from the past to the present and then to the future, incorporating my experiences and interests, which span ages, genres and continents. We looked to the past in its overall postmodernist design, with pointed mid-century items, intricately forged metal pieces, ancient works, organic timber, vintage rugs from North Africa. In the present, we prioritized contemporary design, carefully and painstakingly curating art from Nigeria and all over Africa. And finally, the future is in the architecture and the building itself, a stunning breakthrough moment for architecture in Lagos.

Reading through this book you will find a distinct contemporary language that is SAOTA: bold and innovative, seamlessly but strongly woven into each location and its landscape, with each house taking on its own unique experience. It was a great pleasure to work with this dynamic group of individuals, whose creativity, innovation, ambition and thoughtfulness helped us achieve a dream home that blended all the elements we love and which continues to surprise and inspire me every day. I hope you will be inspired by the individual stories these magnificent buildings and spaces tell you, remembering that behind each one are stories of people, their hopes and dreams, and the other people, SAOTA, who consistently, generously and brilliantly deliver them.

INTRODUCTION

There is something dramatic, epic and even mystical about Cape Town, the city in which we live and work. Table Mountain, the city's most definitive feature, has a powerful presence that is as much spiritual as it is physical. It is a place maker; it has personality and presence. It is earthy and elemental, a dominant natural force that animates life in the city.

Many of our foundational ideas and beliefs were forged in our home city, especially during SAOTA's first decade of existence in the heady, optimistic and transformative time around the release of Nelson Mandela from prison, the end of apartheid and South Africa's transition to democracy during the 1990s. The new confidence and optimism of those early years allowed us a perspective that was forward-looking, confident, uplifting and innovative, as South Africa rejoined a global conversation about architecture and design.

The ideas we negotiated then have an ongoing resonance in our approach and philosophy. The sense of possibility in the air drove our ambition, while the almost spiritual presence of nature embodied in the mountain kept us from trying to express the new identities that were being forged at the time in buildings conceived as singular objects screaming for attention.

Instead, we approached the often spectacularly beautiful sites on which we worked with discretion, with an idea of opening our designs to the beauty and mystery around them, letting their presence in without artifice.

Our approach had its roots in the fascinating and inspiring examples of regional modernism around the country. Our architectural precedents, however, opened up a world of influence with threads and connections as much with Le Corbusier, Mies van der Rohe and European modernism as with the Case Study Houses and California modernism in the USA, Oscar Niemeyer in Brazil, Luis Barragán in Mexico, Jean-François Zevaco in Morocco, and Paul Rudolph and Gawie Fagan in Cape Town.

In seeking to advance our own architectural traditions and create an innovative, refined architecture from our studio in the shadow of Table Mountain, we came to understand the complexities that inform local identities, the cross-pollination, the myriad variety of shared ideas in a global world. We also developed an understanding of how the best aspects of local context, from the site itself to the unique culture, heritage, materials and craft of a place at a particular time, had the seeds of principles that would resonate anywhere in the world.

Despite the appetite for the look and feel of the designs we created in Cape Town, we had no desire to apply a preconceived 'style' repeatedly in new locations, but rather were driven to discover how the ideas and approaches we forged on home ground might continue to engender new expressions wherever we worked, synthesizing with the traditions there. We wanted every SAOTA design to respond at a visceral level to its context, whether a South African cliff edge, a Swiss lakeside, an American seashore, a Russian steppe, a Middle Eastern oasis or an iconic urban location.

As we increasingly work internationally, we have realized — and strive to harness the insight — the global perspectives at the heart of local perspectives.

Over the years, SAOTA has distilled its philosophy into three core elements: LIGHT SPACE LIFE.

LIGHT brings poetry to architecture. It is the very essence of perception, which is why we tend to see buildings not as objects, but as

SAOTA, ARRCC and OKHA Studio at Hatfield 109, Cape Town, South Africa

forms sculpted in light. The energy that is crucial to human life is also the force that reveals mass and renders form, allowing the observer to perceive colour, texture and space. It creates the atmosphere or ambience of a building, marks the passage of time and the rhythms of nature, connecting the life of a building to life on a planetary scale. Our designs embrace light. It influences the orientation of the architecture and how the buildings open to receive it, as well as how we need to control it and provide shelter from it. In South Africa, especially in Cape Town, we are blessed with fresh, clean sunlight. We strive to let this light in so that the interior spaces of our buildings glow. The brightness and clarity of the light in South Africa demands purity and simplicity in form and detailing. These characteristics remain at the heart of our design DNA wherever in the world we work.

SPACE is one of the most primal and fundamental experiences of being human. Among the most exciting aspects of creating space for life in South Africa, and which has become part of our design DNA, is an understanding of shelter – the most basic conception of what architecture does – defined not so much by walls as by the roof. From an early stage, we had the good fortune to find ourselves presented with exceptionally beautiful sites. Perhaps this is what encouraged our conception of architecture as working with, rather than against, the landscape and the elements, magnifying a connection with the surrounding environment. We like to think of architecture as analogous with a tree – something that provides shelter and a sense of place, but does not interrupt the landscape, seeking to formalize it and 'put a hat on it' without disrupting the experience of it. We design with the whole site in mind, the landscape and the views. Our houses 'live out' and we invite the outside in. We like to design gardens and courtyards to allow nature to come into the building and be a part of the experience. We want the earth to touch our architecture. At the same time as our interior spaces borrow from outside, we strive to create light, fresh and open but carefully layered spaces, which mediate our relationships with the setting and the rest of the house with sensitivity and a light touch. Beauty is a very underrated quality in architecture.

LIFE is the true purpose of a building. Any good building is a celebration of human life, and all good architecture should be concerned with improving quality of life. We live in buildings for most of our lives, constructing relationships and families, learning and playing and living. The quality of these buildings has a profound effect on our ability to imagine a better future, to grow and to make a success of what we do with our lives. It is a key building block for a healthy society. We think of our designs as the stages upon which the dramas of life play out: stages for entertaining, for sharing, for rest, for families and for contemplation. They are the theatres in which people live and flourish. The somewhat obvious point – all too often lost and forgotten – that 'architecture with a capital A' can be complex and challenging without being alienating is central to our work. We want to make architecture that people enjoy and we believe that includes a certain magic, mystery and delight. Attending to functionality should never preclude poetry, so we try to choreograph the unfolding experience of space and setting in a way that brings surprise and delight. The ultimate success of a building rests on the question of whether it positively transforms the lives of its inhabitants. Does it make life better? There is a quality of magic about that. But it need not be radical; it can be gentle and humane.

OCEAN VIEW

Cape Town South Africa

This home in Cape Town's Bantry Bay is positioned on a steep mountain ridge below Lion's Head with 360-degree mountain and sea views, taking in Robben Island to the north and Camps Bay and the Twelve Apostles mountain range to the south. The site borders a national park to the south, so excavation was minimized. The brief required a contemporary, uncluttered and sculptural building. The imperative of maximizing the extensive views had to be carefully balanced with the need for privacy.

Only two storeys of the building are visible above street level, respecting the contours and environmental sensitivity of the site. From the road, monolithic white concrete beams contrast with a thin, delicate zinc roof that appears to hover above the light glazed façades of the upper level.

The main living areas, pool terrace and garden are located on the lower of the two levels. The bedrooms are positioned on the uppermost level for privacy. The secondary spaces below are concealed by a large north-facing landscaped wall with indigenous planting, rooting the lower levels in the landscape.

The main point of arrival is at a mid-level via the double-volume garage. Sculptural stairs wrap around a central glass lift that leads to the upper levels. Natural light emanates from the glazed entrance area and is refracted through a glass 'light scoop' ceiling.

The open-plan living areas are arranged in a horseshoe around a central kitchen, carefully layered to vary the experience of each space. These large gallery-type living spaces emphasize the magnetism of the site and the presence of the mountains and the sea. Walls and columns have been limited to maximize the view and blur the boundaries between internal and external spaces. A dramatic covered canopy extends to the end of the site, framing views of Clifton, the Twelve Apostles and Lion's Head.

A courtyard between the main living areas breaks up the massing of the building while creating a sheltered space for all seasons. Its suspended 'woven' weathered Cor-Ten screen offers privacy to the bedroom level above, while the water feature reflects dappled light into the adjacent living areas.

Raw materials with varying textures emphasize the contemporary, sculptural nature of the architecture. The custom-designed white concrete finish that predominates was sandblasted to reveal a fine aggregate, highlighting the robust and understated nature of the architecture. Polished concrete floors in both the internal and external living areas ensure seamless continuity.

Opposite The design carefully balances the site's beautiful 360-degree views with the need to maintain privacy and to respect the Table Mountain National Park, which forms the southern boundary of the site.

Following spread The pool terrace enjoys spectacular vistas, with Bantry Bay to the north and the Twelve Apostles to the south. The concrete canopy is brought to the edge of the property, where the views are most dramatic.

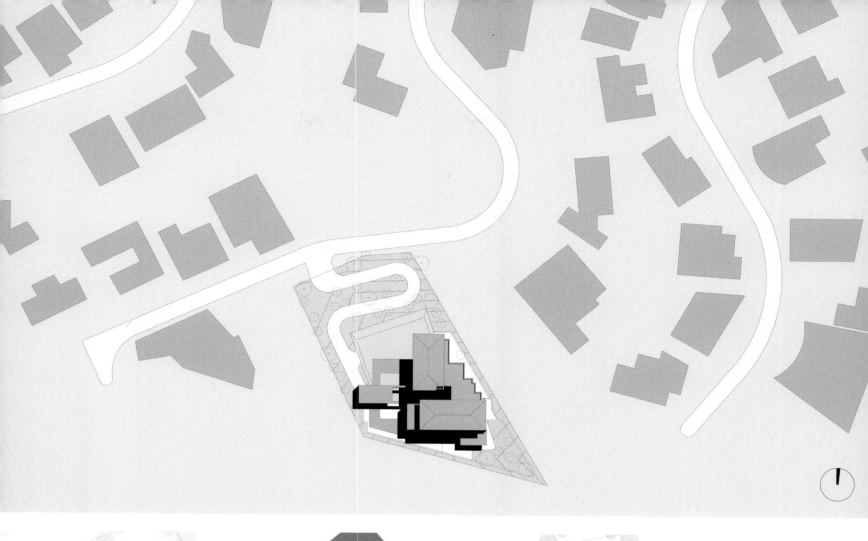

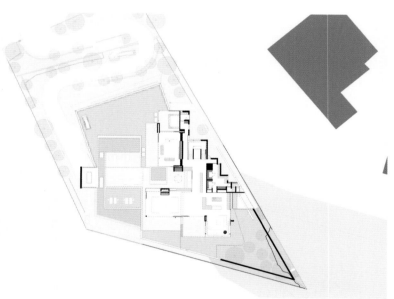

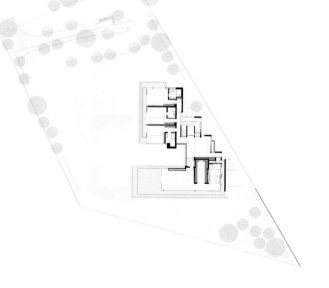

Opposite top The winter lounge with a lower ceiling frames the view, creating an intimate space for more informal gatherings.

Opposite bottom The external Cor-Ten screen suspended in a central courtyard allows patterned light into adjacent living areas. The screen metalwork is by Bad Machine Metalworks.

Top Site plan

Above left Ground floor

Above right First floor

0	10	20m
0	20	40	60ft

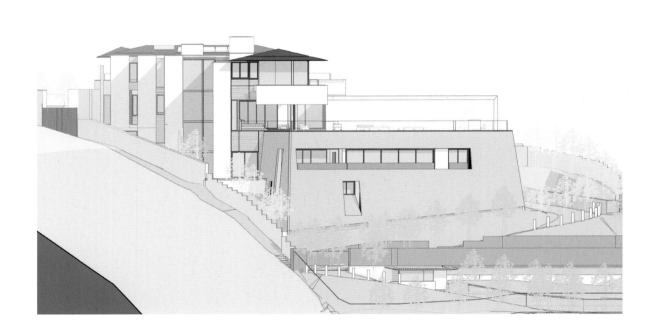

Above right North elevation

Right Section

Opposite, clockwise from top left Suspended woven Cor-Ten sun screen • Graffiti walls in motor court. Artist: Louis Carreon • Internal coffee bar clad in sheet bronze, with counter cast in solid bronze • Sandblasted pre-cast white concrete ceiling beams • Indigenous green vertical garden over lower levels of house • Sandblasted and sealed white concrete wall finish

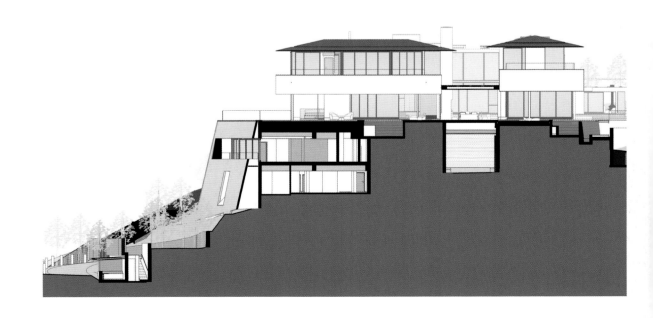

Opposite The central terrace with its suspended woven Cor-Ten screen. The pond reflects patterned sunlight, illuminating the entry and motor court below.

Right The guest bathroom has linear-cut travertine and sandblasted white concrete walls.

Following spread In the summer lounge, sandblasted pre-cast white concrete ceiling beams create continuity, so that the lounge appears a part of both the interior and the exterior of the house.

KLOOF HOUSE

Cape Town   South Africa

This family home is positioned below Lion's Head. With views of Table Mountain, Lion's Head, Signal Hill, the city of Cape Town and the mountains of the Boland and the Winelands in the distance, the architecture is shaped to take in as much of the surrounding area as possible. The strongest gesture is the inverted pyramid roof that creates a clerestory window around the upper level. It allows the building to open up, capturing views of Table Mountain and Lion's Head that would otherwise have been lost. This has also opened up views of the sky, bringing the sun and moon into the home, heightening the connection to nature and its cycles.

The house presents a stone wall to the busy city street, revealing very little about its interior. Its construction is reminiscent of the remains of well-known historical walls around the city, at the Castle or around the harbour, for example. At night the inverted pyramid roof glows, creating a giant lightbox and adding to the intrigue.

One enters the house through the large metal front door, which sits between the house proper and the stone wall, into a small entrance lobby connected to a courtyard garden. From this restrained, quiet space a few steps lead up into the living space, with its bold, cinematic views over the city.

The house is arranged on three levels. The top level has the strongest views and holds most of the living spaces: the open-plan kitchen, dining room and lounge. The family's work and bedroom spaces are on the mid-level, with the garage, gym, cinema and guest room on the lower level.

Each level has its own set of gardens and courtyards. These gardens extend from the mountain surface down against the house, screening the neighbouring buildings and intensifying the relationship with nature, and allowing light and air into spaces that would otherwise be dark and isolated.

The dark exterior breaks down the mass of the building, pushing it into the background. Internally, colours are muted, and the use of a washed oak gives the rooms warmth. The sophisticated spaces are furnished using OKHA furniture.

Opposite From the entrance hall, a few steps ascend into a lobby area that leads through to the living level. This level opens out on to the view of the city and the Boland mountains. The wall sculpture is by Rodan Kane Hart.

Following spread The pool terrace enjoys views of Table Mountain. Decks cantilever over the rim-flow pool, creating lounging space around the swimming pool.

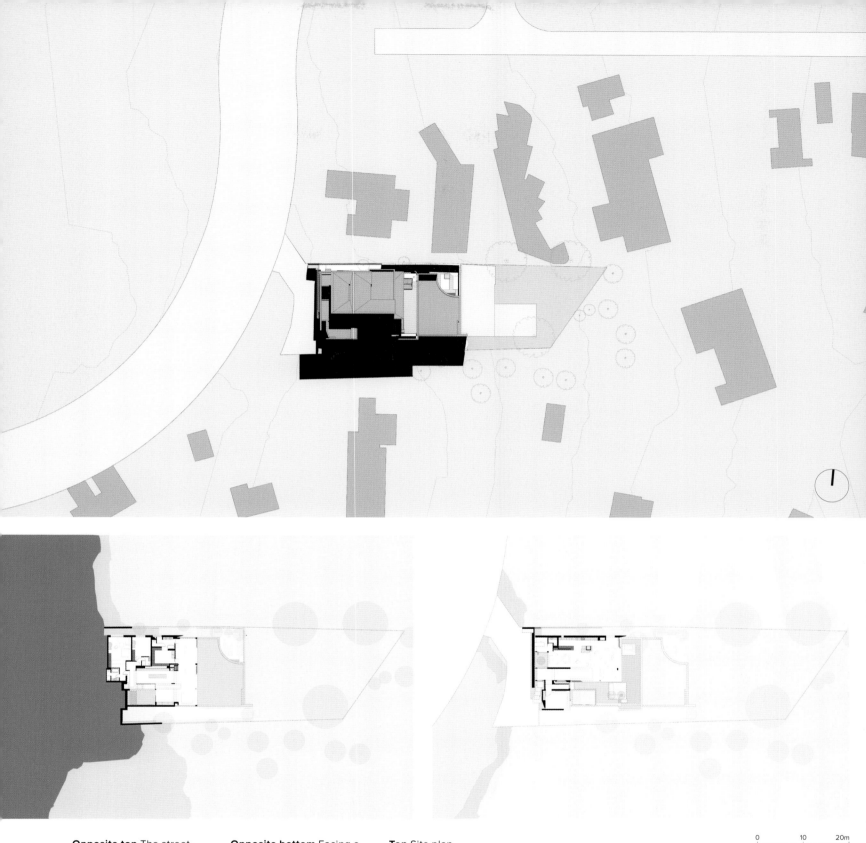

Opposite top The street-facing stone wall at the entrance of the house enters a dialogue with the city's historical urban fabric, referencing some of its earliest buildings.

Opposite bottom Facing a planted courtyard, the study and library area includes a workspace as well as custom shelving and a library ladder.

Top Site plan

Above left Ground floor

Above right First floor

0		10		20m
0	20	40		60ft

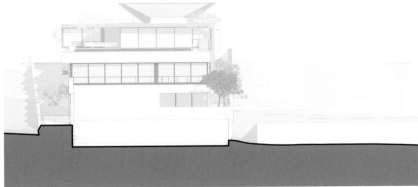

East elevation

North elevation

Below, clockwise from top left Off-shutter concrete wall dividing entrance foyer and dining room • Bathroom screen made from recycled roof beams • Repurposed steel screen from original house • Flamed-granite stairs connecting the main living level and lower level • Flamed-granite entrance stairs referencing the local stone found on the mountains and beaches in Cape Town • Oiled Domex pivot front door • Malmesbury shale stone wall.

Section

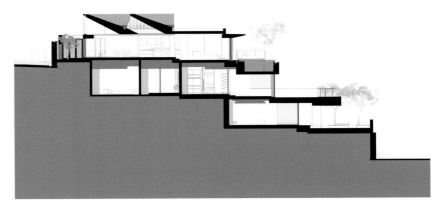

Section

Left The house is entered through a pivoting door, which sits between the house proper and a stone wall.

Opposite A staircase of flamed granite connects the main living level and lower level.

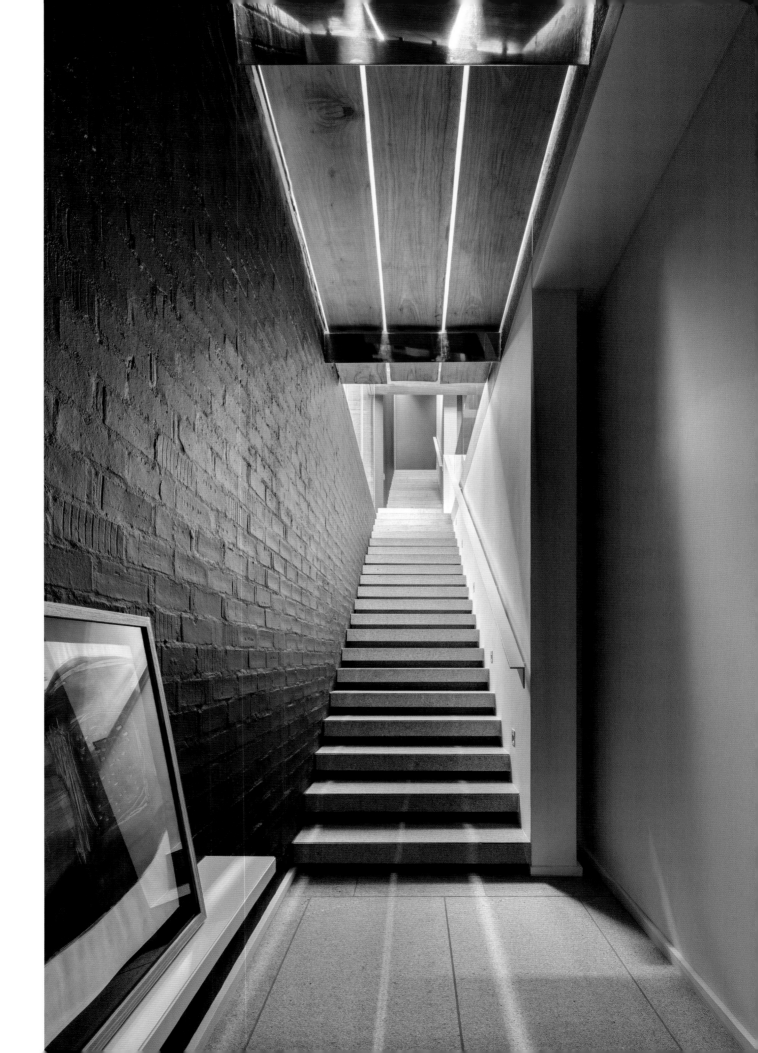

Opposite top Views of Lion's Head through the clerestory windows are created by the inverted pyramid shape of the roof.

Opposite bottom In and around the rooms there are pockets of greenery that evoke a feeling of being surrounded by the landscape.

Right Each level has gardens and courtyards allowing light and ventilation into spaces that would otherwise be dim and enclosed.

Following spread The rim-flow pool blurs the distinction between the architecture and the view over the city. At the same time, the landscaping around the lounge joins the interiors exactly at floor level, creating the impression that the mountain setting cascades right into the room.

BEYOND

Cape Town   South Africa

Perched on the shoulders of Lion's Head, this home springs from a steep hillside that drops off to the famous sequence of Clifton's white beaches to the Twelve Apostles mountain range beyond. Entry from the street gives a carefully composed impression of four lower storeys with tantalizing glimpses of two more levels towering above. The lower levels play host to six generous bedrooms, three of which can be inter-linked for a family suite, and to a double-volume entertainment space complete with spa, games and cinema. Principal living is at the very top of the building – an expansive, double-height, open-plan space that houses kitchen, bar, dining, living and family rooms, as well as a winter lounge, study and art studio at a mezzanine level. The glazed lines between inside and out peel back to blur the boundaries in a con-tinuous transparent space that links a generous back garden, opening directly on to Table Mountain National Park, to a pool that stretches out towards the sea in front.

The entrance façade responds to Le Corbusier's definition of archi-tecture as a 'magnificent play of masses brought together in light' – and the journey through space and light that follows is clearly inspired by the modernist movement. From the cavernous entrance hall with its almost chiaroscuro treatment, the visitor is led upwards towards the generous light of the upper living levels.

The spatial experience is similarly considered: the house feels like a robust, seamless form whose functions are defined by intersecting planes, ceilings and floor treatments. This concept is used from the macro scale of the bar whose glazed form slides dramatically out of the house, floating over the pool with a glass floor, to the material scale of the rough concrete over the main lounge and the timber ceiling on the level below – which, in the true spirit of this house, is made from the very same blemished boards that shuttered the concrete above.

The masterly interplay of light, space and raw materiality in the house plays generous host to its other family – a considered collec-tion of contemporary South African art. The lines between home and gallery are always blurred; and from the Paul Blomkamp tapestry and Paul Edmunds sculpture that animate the mystical entrance hall, to Porky Hefer's playful (and inhabitable) *Blowfish*, which floats within the double-volume entertainment area, and the African masks worked into the dark walls over the kitchen, the collection is always carefully curated to work with the architecture. The interiors were created by ARRCC together with OKHA.

Opposite The double-volume entrance foyer hosts a rusted steel and glass staircase. The artworks are *Three Blind Mice* by Kevin Brand and *Totem* by David Brown.

Following spread The kitchen, dining room, lounge and bar lounge are situated on the fourth floor, with a rim-flow pool that stretches out towards the sea in front. The mask is a Bambara zoomorphic 'Kono' mask; artwork by Martie Kossatz.

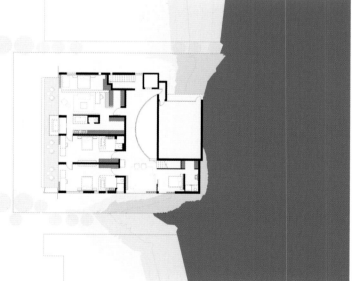

Opposite top The courtyard garden is on the mountain side facing Lion's Head, with distant views of the Atlantic Ocean. The artwork is *Gold and Fish* by Stefan Antoni.

Opposite bottom On the living level the front of house integrates the kitchen and dining room areas. The mask wall features a collection of Central and West African masks. Etch bar stools are by OKHA. The French oak dining table is by Pierre Cronje.

Top Site plan

Above left Third floor

Above right Fourth floor

0 5 10m
0 10 20 30ft

Right Section

Opposite, clockwise from top left Laser-cut aluminium screen inspired by fynbos (scrubland) mountain vegetation • Raw mild-steel side balustrade sheets of staircases left to rust naturally • Malmesbury shale stone rough boundary walls • *Foya*, oiled-steel wall sculpture. Artist: Paul Edmunds • Upcycled raw wood planks reused from casting of concrete ceilings • Off-shutter concrete ceiling with wood grain and blemishes visible

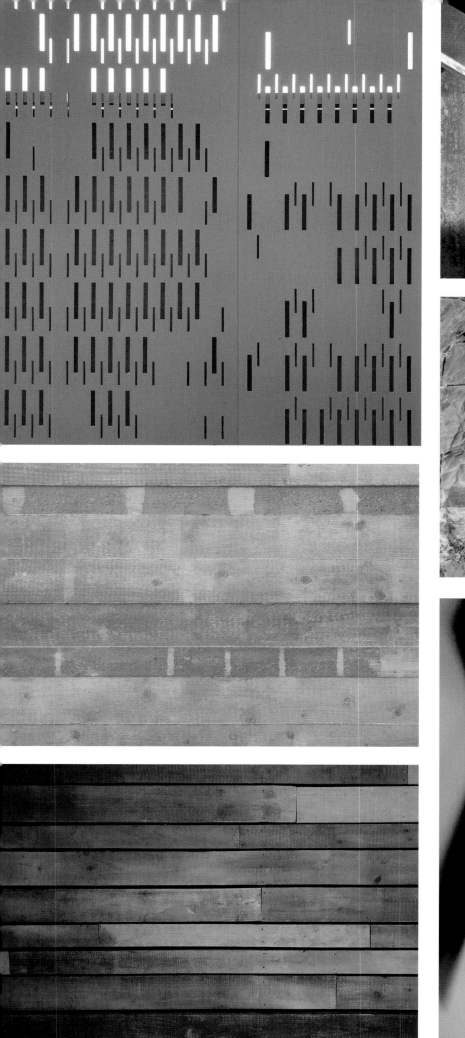

Left The gallery foyer is situated on the bedroom level, with the pyjama lounge at the end. The cinema and games room are on the lower level. The artwork is *Blowfish* by Porky Hefer.

Opposite top In the pyjama lounge two Orgone chairs by Marc Newson sit below the Cloud Lamp by Margie Teeuwen. Artworks are by Charles Gassner.

Opposite bottom The main bedroom incorporates a Bird chair by Harry Bertoia and Jada couch by OKHA, over the Flokati rug; artwork by Yvonne van der Heul.

Following spread The family room is on the far left, with the kitchen, dining room and lounge in the centre. The tapestry is by the Keiskamma Trust. The artworks are a landscape by Andrzej Urbanski and *Nzuri Fufu* by Cyrus Kabiru.

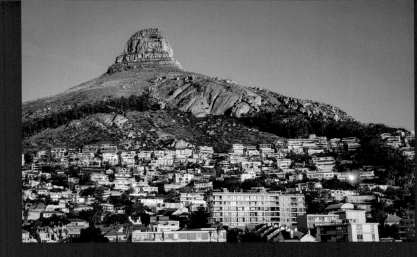

BOMA

Cape Town   South Africa

This Bantry Bay family home on the slopes of Lion's Head overlooks the ocean and has views towards the east of Sea Point, with Robben Island in the distance. The architects' first impulse was to create large open-plan and double-volume spaces with tasked zoning, but the tight site led to a design built over four floors emphasizing the dynamic play of levels.

A redwood and grey-shale façade serves as an understated introduction to the house. The front door opens on to an entrance gallery and courtyard before revealing the soaring volumes and far-reaching views of the ocean-fronting section.

Each zone in the front section has a distinct role while benefiting from the sense of connectivity in an open-plan arrangement. The mood is cocooning and comfortable in the wing housing the family room, its hunkered-down L-shape focusing on the functional living spaces. The living area, however, is as voluminous and dramatic as a contemporary cathedral. Here, a rippling concrete fireplace wall on one end is balanced by a 5-tonne bar of rough-hewn granite on the other. Between them, commanding views animate the grand volume.

This level is configured so that the children are always visible, whether they are outside, watching TV or swimming. Although sea-oriented, with the pool terrace to the west, the living area also leads to a courtyard garden to the east. Sliding glass doors at either end open completely so that it becomes little more than a roof. The pool terrace features a pavilion on either end: a lounging area and a braai-and-dining area.

The bedrooms are one floor down from the living area and the guest and playroom floor in turn is below that. Cut-out shapes and open atrium spaces link the various levels vertically. All three bedrooms lead into one another via sliding doors, so that the children's rooms are easily accessible from the main bedroom. Matching window seats near to the door in each room frame picture-book sea views.

Architecturally, raw textures such as rock, timber and concrete predominate. The interiors create an emotional and sensorial journey in which art plays a pivotal role.

Opposite The house opens on to a courtyard with views towards the east of Sea Point. The sculpture is *Refigure 1* by

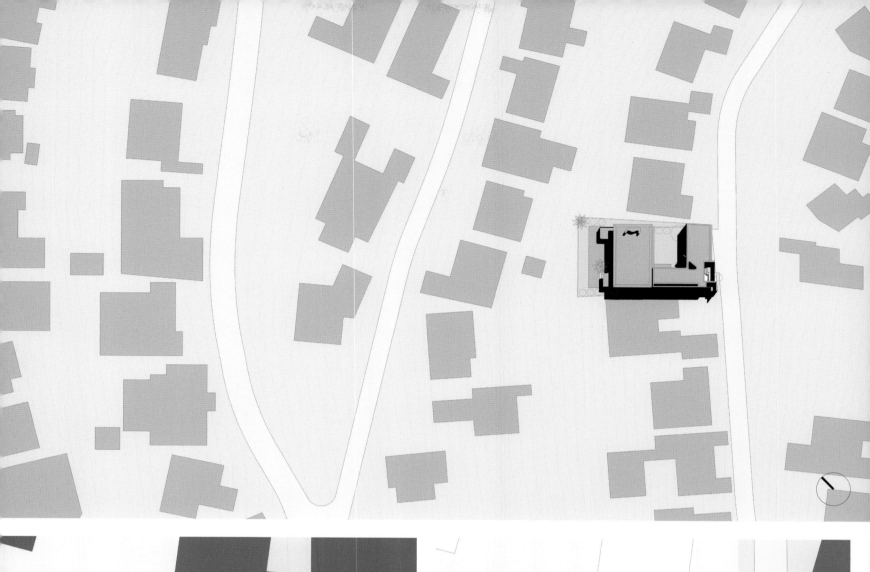

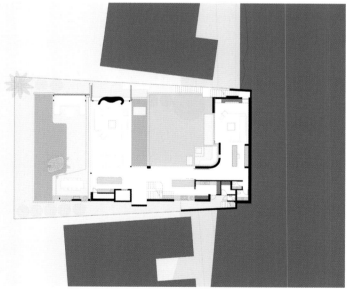

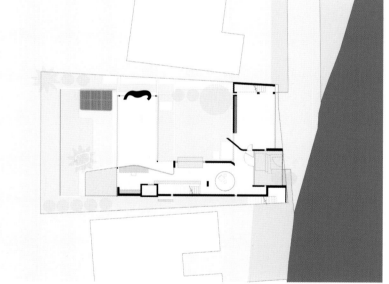

Opposite top The functional living area, with its rippling concrete fireplace, has double-volume living spaces and commanding views.

Opposite bottom The courtyard feels like a natural extension of the adjacent living areas, and when the large sliding doors are opened the threshold is blurred between indoor and outdoor spaces. The sculpture is *Refigure 1* by Anton Smit.

Top Site plan

Above left Second floor

Above right Third floor

0   5   10m
0   10   20   30ft

Below Section

Opposite, clockwise from top left Blue gum slats, limewashed and shaved to expose raw wood finish • Off-shutter concrete fin wall sliding through sheet glass window • Slanted curvilinear off-shutter concrete fireplace wall • Fallen poplar tree trunks, collected and loosely arranged as screen against mirror wall in bathroom • Cape vernacular-style plaster creating uneven surface • Irregular-shaped skylit void

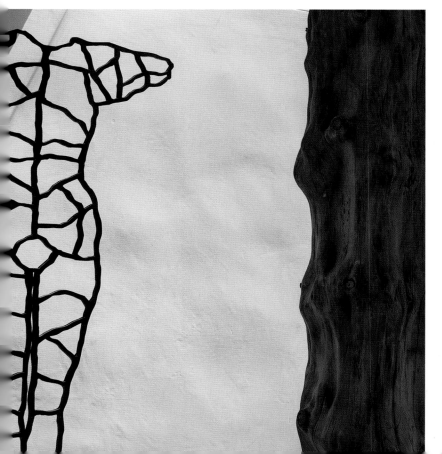

Opposite The concrete staircase has balustrades of thin mild-steel rods that are randomly spaced.

Right The atrium's ceiling is formed of blue gum slats.

Following spread The central courtyard is landscaped to include a boma (firepit area) and a glass-bottomed pond along the edge of the sea-facing living room.

KLOOF 145

Cape Town   South Africa

Accessed from Kloof Road, which winds along the western slopes of Lion's Head, this site is located in the wind-protected suburb of Clifton. The first aspect of the project that required addressing was the steep slope that would have to be excavated to accommodate the structure. The home was conceived as an arrangement of staggered blocks that rise along the side of the mountain, with the upper, private levels becoming appropriately shielded from both visibility and street-level noise.

The conceptual approach to the design was to reinstate the qualities of a natural landscape. The lower part of the building, an independent apartment, is expressed as a heavy stone plinth, its gabion-walled exterior and cocooning interior of dark-stained oak and off-shutter concrete reflecting the strata of the mountainside out of which they emerge. On top of this is a transitional space that is expressed as a green terrace and braai area, representative of what would have been the landscape's foliage level. All levels of the house are connected via a sculptural timber staircase, like a folded ribbon that, appropriate to the home's design narrative, gradually lightens in tone as it rises.

A vertically slatted box hovers over the terrace, allowing the forest bushwillow trees below to grow into this level, with screens that can be opened or closed to adjust the amount of natural light filtering into the interior, lending the effect of being shaded by a large tree. The structure was engineered from a durable yet lightweight aluminium in a finish that mimics the different tones of bark, a durable solution to weathering Cape Town's capricious seasons.

Above this, the living level is set back considerably to follow the slope of the mountain, resulting in added privacy and acoustic buffering while creating the perception that one is on a platform, connected to the surrounding views. The space is visually extended via the introduction of a courtyard towards the mountainside, which allows for ventilation, light and, again, an opportunity for planting. The concrete ceiling of this level is shuttered with rough-sawn planks, championing its raw texture. This emphasis on natural materiality can also be seen in the wooden floors and timber-clad scullery in this space.

The uppermost level, the main bedroom, sits above the tree-tops. The materials — white marble, pale timber — and use of skylights express a feeling of air and openness, while fold-away glass walls welcome in the full expanse of the view.

Opposite The house is an arrangement of staggered blocks rising along the side of the mountain, with upper levels shielded from street-level view.

Following spread The sea-facing aspect of the main living area features an off-shutter concrete ceiling. The rim-flow pool on the living level overlooks Clifton's beaches and the Twelve Apostles mountain range. The artwork is by Jeanne Pfaff.

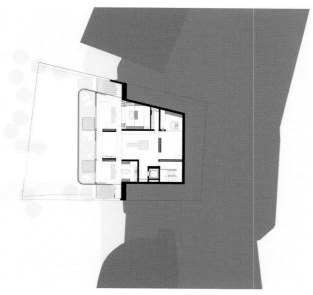

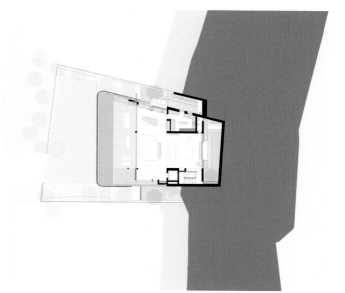

Opposite top The vertically slatted box hovers over the garden terrace, seen here from Kloof Road.

Opposite bottom Interlinking statues by Angus Taylor form a focal point on the garden level, where textured stone leads to an outdoor braai area. The artwork is by Phillemon Hlungwani.

Top Site plan

Above left Third floor

Above right Fourth floor

0   5   10m
0   10   20 30ft

Above right West façade

Right Section

Opposite, clockwise from top left Concrete mosaic and timber finish • Façade screens made of a lightweight aluminium finish conceptually representing tones of bark • Stained oak timber wall and dark timber flooring with grey floor slabs • Quartz and resin wall coating • Dark-stained ash staircase with glass balustrade • Stained oak timber and screed walls

Opposite The staircase is made of dark-stained ash with a glass balustrade. The sculpture is by Dylan Lewis.

Right Lightweight aluminium façade screens can open to offer views over the Atlantic Ocean, or be closed for privacy.

Following spread The timber and glass staircase is backed by a lift shaft clad in beige concrete. Wire-brushed oak floors lend warmth. The sculpture is by Dylan Lewis, artworks by Jeanne Pfaff.

CRESCENT
Cape Town   South Africa

The design for this house in Camps Bay, Cape Town, is primarily a response to site and aspect, creating a dramatic, memorable living space. Apart from a striking and elegant design, the brief also required that the owner should be able to rent out the house either partially or completely. The property, and subsequently the plan of the house, focused on Camps Bay beach and the views of Lion's Head to the north. There are also views back towards the Twelve Apostles and Table Mountain's cable station.

A poorly positioned existing house on the site, which was 50m (164ft) long and 20m (66ft) wide, was demolished, except for a small basement area that was converted into a guest suite. The new double-storey house was positioned centrally, which created a large south-facing front garden. Each level of the house is fully equipped and independently habitable. The upstairs and downstairs sections of the house are very similar, except that the ground floor has a self-contained staff suite and two bedrooms, while the first floor has three bedrooms.

The living spaces are positioned on the northern side of the house, propelling themselves towards the view. They are highly transparent and connect seamlessly with the covered and uncovered terraces. The roof over the deck on the upper level has a steel structure that cantilevers out of the reinforced concrete of the roof slab. A steel ring beam was used to create a cut-out and the remaining external extent of the roof was clad with aluminium panels. Steel sections remain visible, creating the illusion of a very thin roof. Reinforced-concrete upstand beams are set back from the edge of the roof, invisible from below.

The bedrooms are simply arranged off the linear circulation space that forms the rear spine of the house. They look west, taking in the sea views. There is a dramatic staircase in this circulation space with views back towards the cable station.

Clerestory windows along the spine of the house frame views that might otherwise have been missed. Sandblasting of the full-height glazing at the eastern boundary maximizes natural light in the passage and maintains views of the mountain peaks while ensuring the privacy of the neighbouring property.

On the ground floor, a water feature runs the full length of the passage, emphasizing the linearity of the house. At this level, the views from the terrace are mostly restricted to the north. The first-floor terrace, however, is elevated above the neighbouring houses and has 360-degree views.

Opposite The floating roof above the terrace not only provides shelter, but also guides the eye towards the view of Camps Bay beach, while the cut-out frames Lion's Head to the north.

Following spread The striking appearance of the house derives largely from its combination of strong, clean lines and transparency.

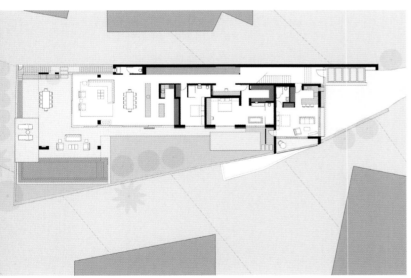

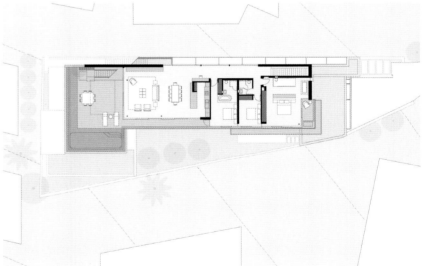

Opposite top The sliding doors of the living areas open away from each other ensuring that internal living effortlessly spills out on to the terraces without interruption. Colours and the choice of materials also play a vital role, with large, elegant porcelain floor tiles being used throughout.

Opposite bottom Even though the furniture is simple and minimal, warmth is introduced through textured fabrics and surface finishes. The colour palette is neutral (soft greys and charcoals), with flashes of bright colour being provided by accent pieces.

Top Site plan

Above left Ground floor

Above right First floor

| 0 | | 5 | | 10m |
| 0 | 10 | 20 | | 30ft |

Left The cantilevered roof with its internal hidden steel support hovers over the rim-flow pool of the external terrace.

Opposite Skylights above the water feature that runs the length of the ground-floor passage allow natural light to flood in and maintain views of the mountain peaks.

Following spread Table Mountain, Cape Town, South Africa.

THE SOUTH AFRICAN HOUSE

Nic Coetzer

ARCHITECTURALLY CONCERNED SOUTH AFRICAN HOUSES – A GENEALOGY AND A GEOGRAPHY

In 1933, South African architect Rex Martienssen met Le Corbusier. Indeed, Corbu might have met his match in someone from 'a distant point in Africa' had the terrible war not ended Martienssen's life some ten years later – quite by accident. Even though his oeuvre was limited to a handful of buildings in and around Johannesburg and Pretoria, this did not stop the painter Fernand Léger from ranking Martienssen as a great pioneer of modern architecture alongside Le Corbusier, Mies van der Rohe, J.J.P. Oud, Alvar Aalto and Frank Lloyd Wright. The meeting they had in Paris was not a minor meeting; Le Corbusier subsequently wrote an inspirational letter to Martienssen that was later published in Le Corbusier's own *Oeuvre complète*. There is a lot of significance in the letter for how we might understand 'the South African house' and how it came to be because it points Martienssen in the regionalist direction Le Corbusier was headed – even if Martienssen did not have time to see it unfold. In fact Le Corbusier's letter to Martienssen calls for an end to rules and schools – he even refers to not following the school of Corbu – and encourages 'fresh proposals from every quarter of the globe' based on an awareness of the beauty and study of nature. Even history is fair game as a source of ideas and inspiration.

> *Study of the past can be fruitful provided we abandon academic teaching and let our curiosity wander across time and space to those civilizations, grandiose or modest, which have expressed human sensibility in a pure form. Architecture must be torn away from the drawing board to fill our hearts and heads – but above all our hearts as proof of our love for it. We must learn to love what is just and sensitive, resourceful and diverse. Reason is only a guide, nothing else.*[1]

The letter ends with an injunction that architecture should bring 'the men of our new mechanical civilization, not just strict utility, but joy itself'. Indeed, there is so much joy in architecture permeating Le Corbusier's work that it is a touchstone for much contemporary architecture – *formally* clear, memorable and sculptured white objects, and *spatially* dynamic, complex and open. From the disciplined classicism

of Villa Savoy to the expressive baroque dynamism of the chapel Notre-Dame du Haut at Ronchamp, it is impossible not to see his work as a high-point of 'classic' modernism, a ghostly white shadow inhabiting our collective psyche.

Prior to Martienssen and the first shadow of Le Corbusier, architect-designed houses in South Africa were largely conceived in what might be loosely called the English tradition. These were generally in a classically inspired idiom, evident in the Cape Dutch revival – best known as 'the Baker School' – mainly found at the Cape or on the northward-looking *koppies* (hillocks) of Johannesburg's Parktown. In the English tradition, houses were typically double-storeyed, insular and cellular, spatially compacted and generally oriented around the fireplace as a heating strategy. To be clear, the Arts and Crafts movement had started a reorientation of domestic architecture towards what we have come to call passive heating and cooling design strategies, as well as a slow loosening of the spatial boundaries of the more public rooms of the house – the work and writing of Raymond Unwin and Barry Parker demonstrate this reorientation. Indeed, some of the work of the Cape Dutch revival had started to engage this loosening strategy, with Herbert Baker himself extolling the virtues of designing to climate and geography; and in the South African context, this orientation had started to shift outwards towards a covered stoep, or loggia. Apart from the introduction of a covered stoep, the South African house was, prior to Martienssen and Le Corbusier, essentially a collection of boxes held within a bigger box that did not have any significant relationship with its immediate environment, climate or geography or, indeed, any of the other spaces in the house.

Ironically, Martienssen's house designs (fig. 1, House Stern), and those of the Transvaal Group including Norman Hanson (fig. 2, Denise Scott Brown's childhood home; and fig. 8, House Harris) and Gordon McIntosh (fig. 3, House Munro), repeated this approach, with stripped-down, white prismatic boxes as reworkings of Le Corbusier's own idiom, particularly in his Villa Stein; these were objects gleaming in the Highveld sun, brilliant and somewhat emphatic – sculptural but not necessarily easily inhabited. The importance of Martienssen – and by proxy, Le Corbusier – lives on in what might be referred to as

architecturally concerned South African houses, although not necessarily through the example of Martienssen's designs (fig. 4, House Martienssen). In his brief time as an architect and the short thirty-seven years of his life, Martienssen was a lecturer at and later head of Wits University's school of architecture, where he concluded a PhD, became editor of the *South African Architectural Record* and was elected president of the Transvaal Provincial Institute of Architects. It was through these roles and institutions that Martienssen doggedly promoted the modern movement in architecture and, in particular, the work and ideas of Le Corbusier. But the ending of the Second World War can in some ways also be understood as the end of a particular kind of avant-garde and utopian modernism that demanded an emphatic break with the past. As modernism spread through the world the *esprit nouveau* softened as it encountered other kinds of geographies, climates, cultures and traditions. Indeed, Colin St John Wilson has written about 'the other tradition of modern architecture', in the book of that name, that started to gain traction after the ideologues of the 1920s and 1930s gave way to a more regionally based and less rule-based exploration of architectural modernism. This is exactly the evolution and open attitude that Le Corbusier had expressed in his letter to Martienssen.

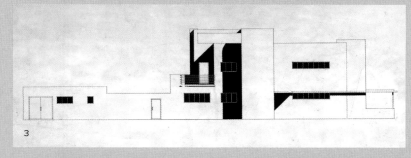

After Martienssen, South African modernism was very quickly imbued with a regionalist sensibility – albeit with the work of Le Corbusier as the touchstone to which design referred. The new school of architecture at Pretoria, established in 1943, continued the ethos of the modern movement but with a stronger regionalist stance – not only in terms of climate but also in terms of local building materials and buildability. The post-war period aligned modernism's functionalism with a concern for frugality in building materials and their clever and optimal use. The monopitch corrugated-iron roof with windows aligned to rafter or truss spacings quickly became a recurring trope in domestic architecture and replaced the earlier experiments in flat concrete roofs that were deemed to have failed in the harsh Highveld sun. Careful solar orientation and large overhangs with access to generous veranda spaces became dominant in a renewed concern for thermal comfort and liveability. This was typified with a shallow plan depth to

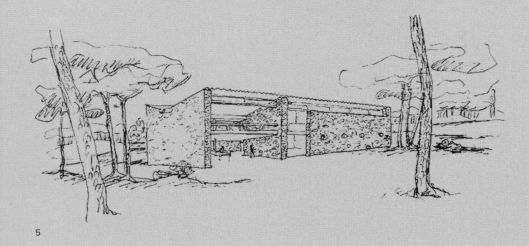

5

6

7

8

maximize light and cross-ventilation but also a general flattening of houses as horizontally spreading forms and spaces flowing from inside to outside, with subtle spatial shifts breaking out of the box of cellular spaces. On top of that, Le Corbusier himself had given the all-clear for experiments in building materials – shifting away from the white plastic formalism of the early stages of the modern movement – in his design for a house at Mathes in France (fig. 5, Villa 'Le Sextant'). The result was more restrained than Frank Lloyd Wright's Arts and Crafts abundant articulation, and was a simplified and essentialist approach to building materials as being fundamental to their character as wall, floor or roof and their primacy in the spatial definition of the design. If the early modern movement had fixated on the articulation of the exterior formal mass as an asymmetrical composition – as justified through functionalist rhetoric – then the South African regionalist response shifted half of the interest and care back to the interior and its inhabitation looking outward. The regionalist shift also resulted in a lasting experiment with crazy paving and slasto...

A similar pattern also emerged halfway across the world in California. The same delayed engagement with the purist modern movement allowed a more forgiving regionalist response in the work of Rudolph Schindler and Richard Neutra as well as in the various Case Study houses – such as Pierre Koenig's iconic Stahl House (figs 6 and 7). Like South Africa's emerging regionalist modernism, the California variant showed a similar concern for the simplified and elemental use of building materials and structure, capturing the new spirit of informal living with an easy-going set of open-plan relationships – though not the kitchen, not yet – and indoor–outdoor veranda or terrace spaces. The climatic parallels between the Highveld and California in many ways explain the similarities in the emergent regionalist modernist architectures despite it being 15,000km (9,300 miles) away. But beyond the climate, the houses demonstrate an emergent relaxed approach to living, an outward-looking and open attitude to life that was a significant shift away from the inward-looking, insular and cellular structure that had defined the English house and its domestic space. The shift from Arts and Crafts sensibilities to regionalist modernism can be identified in the shift from the dominance of the hearth in the work of Frank Lloyd Wright to the dominance of the terrace in the work of Richard Neutra.

If the architecturally concerned South African house is made in the white prismatic shadow of Le Corbusier – but as a regionalist variant – then it might be helpful to consider if there are any shifts across the general climatic and geographical regions of South Africa. This could be simplified into those on the Highveld and including the plains of the Free State *platteland*, to the steaming subtropical hills of KwaZulu-Natal and surrounds, and to the mountainous and windy Cape. A few examples might illustrate how architects responded to these different regions and where the commonalities and differences lie.

The grid-framed, low monopitch of the Highveld

There is not much wind on the high inland plateau of the Highveld. Days are still, cold and crisp in winter but brilliantly sunny to bake up a well-placed veranda by mid-morning. Summer days are hot and dry – but not excessively so – and are relieved by occasional after-noon thunderstorms. The regionalist modernism that emerged in and around Johannesburg and Pretoria was appropriately without drama and veered towards a functional and rational coherence between structure, plan and building materials. Perhaps it was the establishment of the state-owned steel manufacturer ISKOR in the area that set the use of steel posts, corrugated-iron roofs and modular steel windows as design determinants – especially in the low-rust dry air. This is clearly evident in the work of Hellmut Stauch, a lecturer at the newly established school of architecture at the University of Pretoria. The rationalizing of the plan with a 1m (3ft) framed grid – with the roof structure exposed across the ceiling running from the dominant north-facing windows to the back of the space – continued into the section where volumes were determined according to function, with the living room enjoying an expanded volume and bedrooms tight-ened, while overhangs were calibrated to control solar gain. Already in the 1940s, Stauch was extolling the virtues of butterfly (V-shaped) roofs as a rational solution for bringing space, light and air movement to where they were most needed (figs 9–11, Dundee Town Council House Types; and figs 13–15, Winckley House).

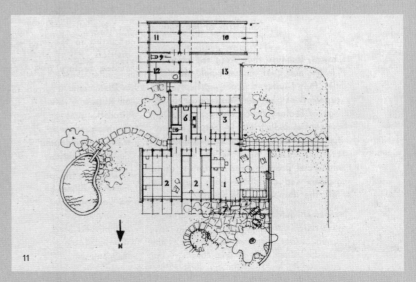

The same elements were used in the later work of Norman Eaton, especially in his Greenwood and Anderssen houses, in the Willows outside of Pretoria (fig. 16, House Greenwood). Eaton's work is generally considered to be much more experimental in terms of building materials and their possible 'African' rootedness than Stauch's more systems-oriented approach. Eaton is perhaps most famous for his Netherlands Bank building in Durban and its exquisite veil of turquoise ceramic breeze blocks. But in the Greenwood and Anderssen houses he follows a rationalist approach to a north orientation as well as creating a systemized structure that informs and drives the window and sliding door rhythm. The joy is in the careful detailing of local materials such as stone from the site and a brick paving pattern that recalls Roberto Burle Marx – through this, Eaton took hold of the entire site, making it an expressive counterpoint to the formal clarity of the house. The joy of making and crafting an interior comes through in various detail drawings such as breeze-block screen walls and a custom front-door handle. The work is more spatially complex than Stauch's systemized response, with the Greenwood house having a higher-level study over the dining room that also creates a 'loggia' on the roof as it is accessed by a separated staircase turret.

The endless veranda of KZN

The breeze off the Indian Ocean is a welcome relief in the sweltering summer nights of the subtropics of KwaZulu-Natal. Cross-ventilation is everything, anything to shift the humid air around and bring some relief from the mosquitoes in the lush jungle vegetation. On the other hand, winter days are mild and sunny. An endless veranda becomes the key asset to shelter the walls from the sun and rain in the summer but also to provide escape from the warmer interior spaces of the house in the evening.

University of Natal professor Barry Biermann's own house (fig. 12, House Biermann) in Durban formed a broad U-plan shape that cascades down the slope with a single unifying concrete roof that also covers the veranda edge of the U. True to the breezy requirements of the climate, the circulation from living to sleeping areas is outside, under this overhanging shelter as if down a sloping cloistered walkway

– revealing a sequence of staged architectural encounters across the open central garden. There are other real joys in this house, from the contrasting curvilinear garden walls that are a counterpoint to the U to the light cannons that bring a surreal yellow glow to the interior. Most memorable is the somewhat ad-hoc collection of Victorian bric-a-brac building components such as cast-iron filigree, cast-iron columns and some free-floating stained-glass windows that act as a softening addition to the more severe Corbusian aspects of white-painted bagged walls. Even at the front door mystery abounds, with the 'porch' of reclaimed Victorian cast-iron filigree and an intensely modulated and erratically textured white wall. With its collection of sculptures and other African artefacts, House Biermann acts as a local and externally oriented version of John Soane's home in London, which is a rich and unfolding experiential tour-de-force. Barry Biermann was an academic, a provocateur and a collector of handmade things. He inspired a generation of Natal-educated architects to take history seriously, but also to take their immediate context and locale seriously, to take the richness of Africa seriously and to read the modern movement as a reinventing potential within that context. The result, evident in his own home, was a set of localized intensities set within an overall formal-spatial design strategy – harmonic notes across the dominant theme. Biermann was a brilliant scholar of history, local architecture and modernism; his house can easily be read as an amalgam of Cape Dutch formal singularities, dispersed Victorian multiplicities and African architectural influences all held together within a modernist spatiality akin to Le Corbusier's 'architectural promenade'.

The sculpted surfaces of the Cape

If we did not know better we might think that the wind had carved the great mountains of the Cape – such is the power of its presence. But while there is a little truth to this, the opposite is more significant: the mountains carve the wind out. With the dominant, strong summer south-easter and the stormy winter north-wester, the Cape mountains add more drama by creating windward and leeward sides in reverse order of the seasons. This causes localized gale-force winds on the leeward side as the wind whips around and over the mountains to fill

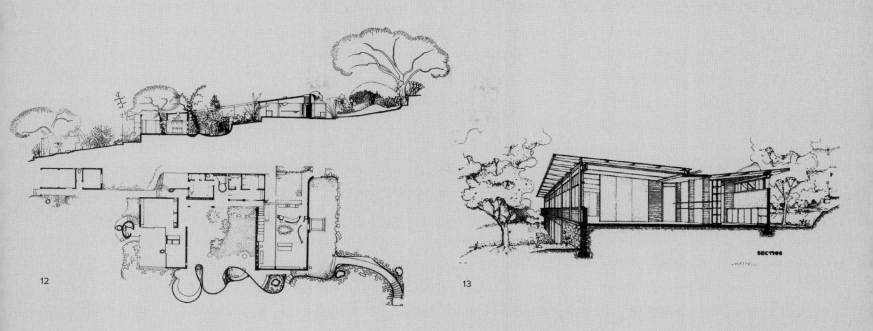

12

13

the vacuum, while areas just over the mountains on the windward side experience the same wind as a gentle breeze. At the Cape, the wind and the mountains are truly dramatic counterparts. On top of that, the winter storms can be ferocious, driving rain nearly horizontally under just about any overhang. Whatever climate change might bring, it is still the 'Cape of Storms'.

It is hardly surprising then, that the modernist regionalism of the Cape from the likes of Gawie Fagan and Revel Fox makes reference to the original settler architecture known as Cape Dutch, which perversely struck a defiant boxy objectness to the elemental drama of the Cape. This settler vernacular combined classical elements from northern Europe – such as ornately gabled entrances – with limited local building materials. These comprised sun-dried brick or rubble walls with a whitewashed hand-plastered mud finish. This formed a strong contrast against the downy and dark thatch roof, and was also a stark counterpoint to the mountains that surrounded these object-buildings. Up close though, the whitewashed and handmade walls become alive with a range of blue and purple hues and tones as the subtle changes in surface direction pick up reflected light from adjacent areas.

For an architect trained in the glimmering white shadow of Le Corbusier – as Gawie Fagan was at the University of Pretoria – the Cape Dutch homesteads were ready-made local variants of the iconic plastic forms that Le Corbusier conjured. As Corbu himself said, 'Architecture is the masterly, correct and magnificent play of masses brought together in light', and the light of the Cape is an abundant resource for this. In Fagan's domestic architecture it is rare to come across a wall surface that is not whitewashed, while the bagged brick walls afford a similar rendition of light to that of the original handmade Cape Dutch wall surface. This approach to craft and the crafting of surfaces and smaller built elements comes across in the iconic and influential Die Es (fig. 17, Die Es), Fagan's own home in Camps Bay, which he and his family famously built with their own hands. The house's name, 'the hearth', in reference to the oversized iconic sculptural form, hints at the prevalence of Cape Dutch tropes in Fagan's work (fig. 19, Die Es). Indeed, the house has a more bounded form that hunkers

14

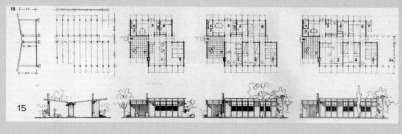

15

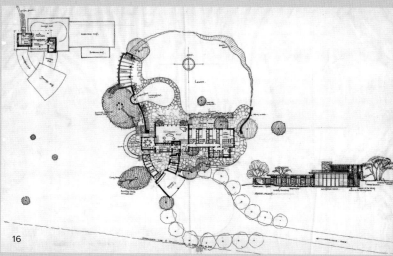

16

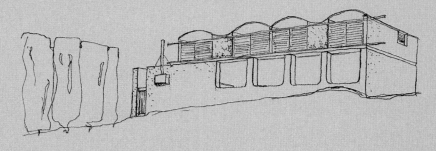

17

down against the summer south-easter that wages dramatic warfare down the slopes of Camps Bay. The large sliding-door windows of the main living space bear witness to this and are heightened by the singular starkness of the quarry-tile floor and the off-shutter concrete ceiling, while on the upper bedroom level the roof swoops a concave-convex wooden vault against the wind. Die Es is a peaceful cave from which to live the drama of the Cape of Storms, staging just the right amount of control and engagement with the elements as and when needed, and in the colder climate of the Cape, bringing inhabitation partially back to the hearth.

Elemental dramas in the architecture of SAOTA
Table Mountain is largely made up of sandstone layers. In parts, some bands form shallow, broad caves from which the world can be surveyed, helping to make these places of both refuge and prospect, of safety but also openness. All this while the ferocious summer south-easter rages the tablecloth of clouds down on Table Mountain.

This is the elemental drama that truly defines the domestic architecture of SAOTA, an architecture that works incredibly hard to be as vital as the earth itself. While the firm builds more and more abroad, it is in and around the slopes of Table Mountain that the practice was born and has come to be masterly. It is on this dramatic terrain that the domestic architecture of SAOTA first continued the explorations of space and light initiated by Rex Martienssen through Le Corbusier – perhaps best seen in the earlier works of Stefan Antoni Architects, which held their own as beautifully sculpted, John Lautner-inspired curvilinear objects set upon the land, similar in some ways to Cape Dutch homesteads (fig. 18, Buffelsdrift Farm). While other architecturally concerned South African practices are held to the delimiting strictures of the Pretoria school and its systemized and economical approach to structure, building materials and window and door openings, SAOTA's clients have given them room to explore the more haptic and formally and spatially complex responses to site and light and material that were perhaps started with Norman Eaton, Barrie Biermann and Gawie Fagan – and with a good measure of Richard Neutra or Pierre Koenig to help make things disappear. Where earlier South African regionalist

modernism used expanses of glass to capture light and views, with SAOTA the wall of glass disappears, and the space of life and living is held under an emphatic protecting roof. This dematerialization of boundaries and boxes not only allows a flow of space from mountain to sea – the passage of life temporarily held and stilled under the protecting roof – but also enables a set of unfolding platforms and spaces where the little and big dramas, joys and pleasures of life can be held with ease and generosity, an extraordinary stage set for life. This strategy of an emphatic roof – the sky rendered as a protective plane held up as if by magic while spaces accumulate underneath in apparently casual eddies – also opens the houses up to powerful diagonal vistas that shift perspectives and reveal deliberately layered spatial complexities, a sculpted space of terraces and platforms that is the inverse of the inward-focusing box-and-hearth of earlier times, a free-roaming 'architectural promenade'.

This is the work of inhabiting a sandstone cave, a gradation of refuge and prospect from a point of safety and protection, as giant sliding doors open the inside to a continuity of veranda and the expansive horizon. This haptic sensibility is continued through in more complex formal and spatial interplay, with light that brings the interior alive with dramatic moments of illuminated texture and surface – at times the cave analogy is intensified as the ceiling plane is articulated through timber or darker surface materials. Design continues through to the careful detailing of materials and their interaction with light, space and form – everything is considered, engaged with, optimized and made luxuriant through an exacting craftsmanship. This is the work of a firm that is at the level of top practices around the world and with staff and directors who are endlessly finding the joy in architecture and finding out what architecture can do. As they galvanize their practice through the words 'light space life' they give their clients the gift of architecture: of what Le Corbusier calls 'joy itself'.

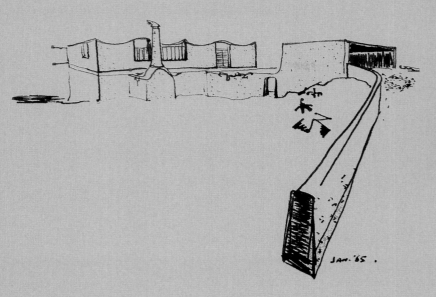

Fig. 1 House Stern, Johannesburg, South Africa, by Rex Martienssen (1934). Image from 'The Genesis of a House' by Kurt Jonas, *South African Architectural Record*, March 1937. Photographer: George Abbott. Courtesy: Architecture Archives at the University of Pretoria (AAUP)

Fig. 2 Denise Scott Brown's childhood home, Johannesburg, South Africa, by Norman Hanson (1934). Photograph: Denise Scott Brown. Courtesy: Denise Scott Brown

Fig. 3 House Munro, Pretoria, South Africa, by Gordon McIntosh (*c*.1931). Courtesy: Architecture Archives at the University of Pretoria (AAUP)

Fig. 4 House Martienssen, Johannesburg, South Africa, by Rex Martienssen (1939). Courtesy: Architecture Archives at the University of Pretoria (AAUP) and Herbert Prins Collection

Fig. 5 Villa 'Le Sextant', France, by Le Corbusier (1935) © FLC-ADAGP. Plan FLC 8397

Fig. 6 Stahl House, Los Angeles, USA, by Pierre Koenig (1960). Image © J. Paul Getty Trust. Getty Research Institute, Los Angeles (2004.R.10)

Fig. 7 Stahl House, Los Angeles, USA, by Pierre Koenig (1960). Image © J. Paul Getty Trust. Getty Research Institute, Los Angeles (2004.R.10)

Fig. 8 House Harris, Johannesburg, South Africa, by Norman Hanson (1933). Image from 'The Small House in Modern South African Architecture' by Alan Lipman, *Lantern*, December 1962. Courtesy: Architecture Archives at the University of Pretoria (AAUP)

Fig. 9 – Fig. 11 Dundee Town Council House Types by Hellmut Stauch (1945). Images/drawings courtesy of SVA International

Fig. 12 House Biermann, 38 Glenwood Drive, Durban, South Africa, by Barrie Biermann (1962). Image from 'Architect's House, Durban (1962–)' by Barrie Biermann, *UIA Journal*, Issue 8/1985, 46–47

Fig. 13 – Fig. 15 Winckley House, Pretoria, South Africa, by Hellmut Stauch (*c*.1941). Images/drawings courtesy of SVA International

Fig. 16 House Greenwood, Pretoria, South Africa by Norman Eaton (1950). Courtesy: Norman Eaton Collection, Architecture Archives at the University of Pretoria (AAUP)

Fig. 17 Die Es, Camps Bay, Cape Town, South Africa, by Gawie Fagan (1965), initial thumbnail sketch. Courtesy: Gabriel Fagan Architects

Fig. 18 Buffelsdrift Farm, Ladismith, South Africa, by Jaco Booyens Architect and SAOTA (2019). Photograph by Adam Letch

Fig. 19 Die Es, Camps Bay, Cape Town, South Africa, by Gawie Fagan (1965). Courtesy: Gabriel Fagan Architects. Photograph by Gawie Fagan

Endnote

1 Le Corbusier and Pierre Jeanneret, *Oeuvre complète de 1910–1929*, Zürich: Dr H. Girsberger, 1943

SILVER BAY

Shelley Point   South Africa

This holiday home at Shelley Point on the West Coast Peninsula was designed for a young family with space for guests. The site is positioned on the northern tip of the peninsula on a small spur of land that juts into the Atlantic with west-, north- and east-facing beaches. Unusually for the West Coast, the site faces east, overlooking the bay towards the mountains behind the Swartland town of Aurora.

The bay is home to Heaviside's dolphins and southern right whales and is an important stopping point for migratory birds. The climate is warm and dry and is characterized by strong south-easterly winds in summer and north-westerly winds in winter. The site slopes from west to east, from the street to the beach.

The design of the house was strongly influenced by three key contextual conditions. First, the elevated entrance prompted the decision to situate the living spaces on the upper level and the bedrooms and playroom below, enabling views of the bay and the water's edge from the living spaces. Second, the prevailing wind coming in from the south-east necessitated large glazed sliding doors to provide shelter while maximizing the view in the same direction. The third challenge was the question of how to let northern sun into the interior of the house. The pool was positioned in a courtyard on the northern face, which not only allows in the sunlight, but also creates a wind-free outdoor area year-round regardless of the wind direction.

The upper floor was conceptualized as a continuous L-shaped space pivoting around a conical flue made from Cor-Ten steel and embracing the pool courtyard. It includes an entrance hall and kitchen, dining and living areas, each given a distinct identity with changes in level.

The thatched roof is supported by a perimeter I-beam and steel tie rods, which allow its open volume. Off-shutter concrete slabs form the ceiling on the lower level. The stair is also made from I-beams, with 75mm- (3in-) thick eucalyptus planks forming the treads.

The simple cellular bedrooms have a serrated façade with corner glazing to maximize the views. Glass walls separate the en-suites from the bedrooms, allowing the two spaces to share a larger volume.

The interior is a sophisticated and eclectic mix of laid-back, comfortable and robust furniture. Natural timber and charcoal and grey fabrics are accented with washed-out red patchwork kilims and blue log stools, layered with natural materials and textures such as grass-cloth wall coverings and woven baskets. Proportions are over-scaled and inviting. Large sofas are nested with clusters of cushions and throws, instantly reflecting an easy-going holiday lifestyle.

Opposite Sliding aluminium and glass doors lead on to a wind-protected courtyard on the north side of the house.

Following spread A timber walkway at the side of the house offers direct beach access, and the Shelley Point Lighthouse is a feature of the extensive views. The house's indigenous fynbos (scrubland) garden blends into the natural coastal landscape.

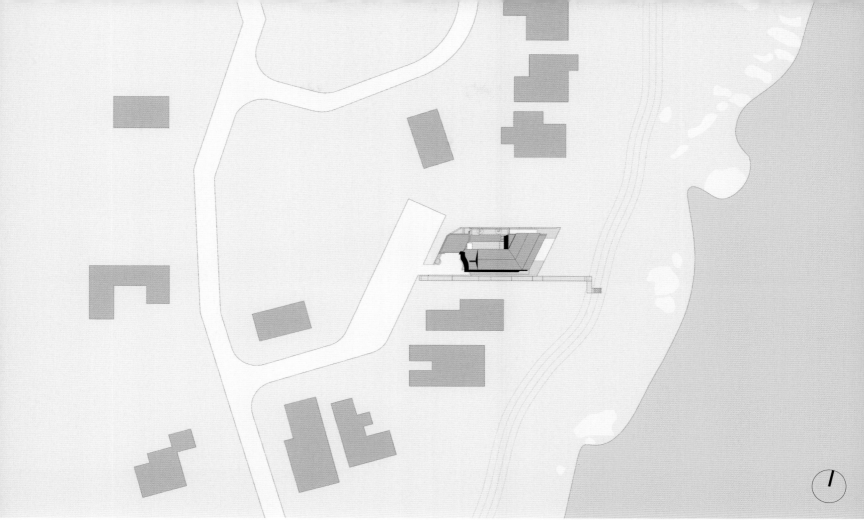

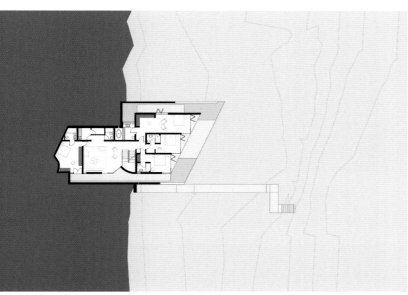

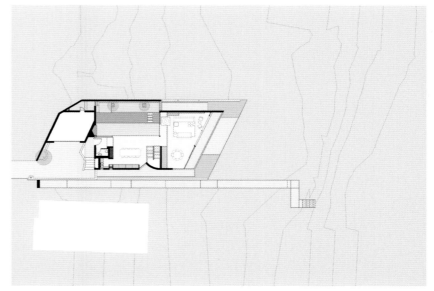

Opposite top The living spaces are on the first floor, allowing for views of the bay as well as the water's edge.

Opposite bottom The elevated entrance on the first floor incorporates a SAOTA-designed Cor-Ten steel entrance wall panel. Screen metalwork is by Bad Machine Metalworks.

Top Site plan

Above left Ground floor

Above right First floor

0   5   10m
0   10   20 30ft

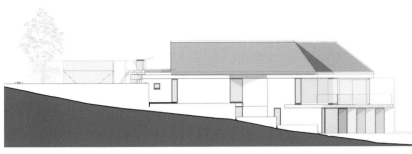

North elevation

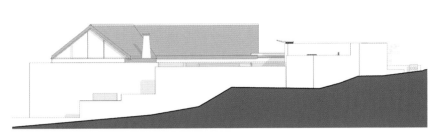

South elevation

Below, clockwise from left Pitched thatch roof with glazed gable · Conical fireplace flue of Cor-Ten steel · Cor-Ten steel entrance wall panel · Off-shutter concrete ceiling slabs · Thatched roof fixed to gum tree laths and pole rafters · Flamed-granite bathroom floor with found pebbles · Meranti timber wind screen to courtyard

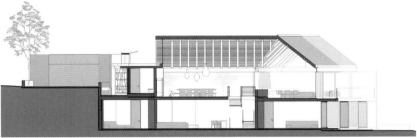

Section

Section

Opposite top The sheltered courtyard provides an extension to the single-space living area of the upper level.

Opposite bottom The pitched thatch roof is supported by a big steel I-beam; steel tie rods are used to create an expansive, double-volume space.

Right Custom wrought-iron lights were created for the kitchen. Metalwork is by Bad Machine Metalworks.

Following spread The first floor has been conceptualized as a single space holding the north-facing pool courtyard, bordered by the kitchen with a large table, and a dining and living space on the eastern edge.

ULUWATU

Bali   Indonesia

This getaway home in Uluwatu, on the south-western tip of the Bukit Peninsula of Bali, Indonesia, is dramatically perched on a limestone cliff edge with elevated ocean views. The large east–west-oriented site faces the ocean on the eastern side. The generous scale of the site allowed for a resort-inspired layout with separate suites and living spaces in a fragmented arrangement that weaves together indoor and outdoor spaces.

A series of courtyards, gardens and other planted terraces is woven into the architecture, integrating landscape and structures. The design was partly inspired by the way in which rocky ruins are, in time, reclaimed by landscape, and come to seem almost as if they are part of it.

A large palm-lined entry courtyard creates a dramatic sense of arrival, with a grand staircase floating over a cascading water feature. Monolithic stone-clad walls add a singular design statement to the central entrance. Lounge, dining room and a covered terrace form the core of the cellular arrangement of buildings and pavilions, which radiate outwards. A large courtyard to the west provides an enclosed counterpoint to the vast views to the east.

Throughout the plan, sizeable spaces such as the entrance, pool terrace and western courtyard are balanced with intimately proportioned living spaces. Various courtyards, pavilions and terraces offer a variety of outdoor experiences with varying degrees of cover. The porous nature of the design encourages naturally cooling cross-ventilation to flow in from the ocean.

Aesthetically and stylistically, SAOTA took inspiration from Balinese architecture's unique hybrid of mass and lightweight elements, evident in traditional temples as much as in contemporary buildings. The monumental mass walls at the entrance, for example, contrast with the main living areas, where the vernacular timber pavilions have been reinterpreted using glass curtain walling, and the local lightweight timber roofs have been re-envisioned as a floating concrete form crafted with board-marked concrete. The slope of the roof invites in the morning light and opens up ocean views to the east, while providing shelter from the harsh western afternoon light.

Throughout the house, the texture of the concrete and natural finishes such as local stone have been overlaid with distinctive timberwork. Vertical screens, joinery and decorative metalwork enrich the raw materiality with thoughtful details. Honed and unfilled travertine floors provide a luxurious finish underfoot, while the continuity of the finishes imparts a sense of calmness and cohesion.

Architect of record: H+H Architecture

Opposite Interior and exterior spaces are interwoven, encouraging indoor–outdoor living.

Following spread Local black andesite stone with 45-degree hand-chiselled grooves is used for walls. A flight of travertine steps creates a waterfall at the entrance to the home.

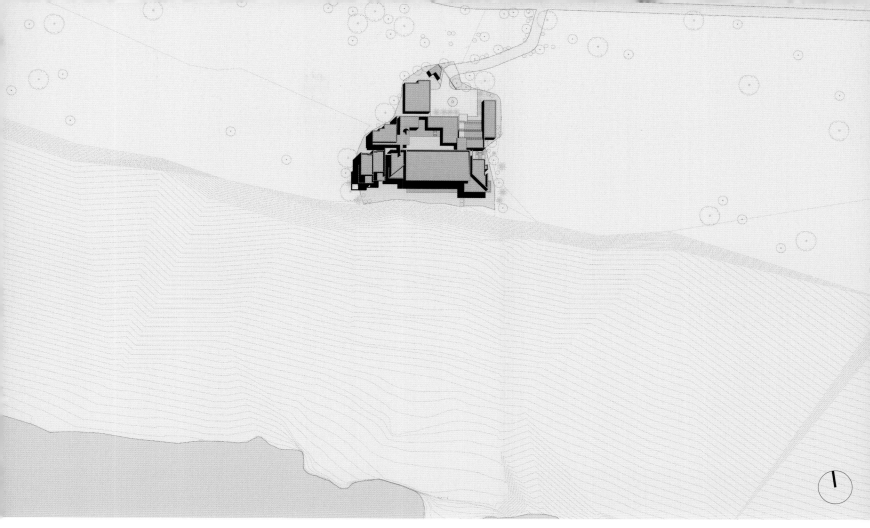

Previous spread The courtyard is bordered with palm and frangipani trees, which stand before the vertical face of the monolithic concrete roof.

Opposite top left The floating concrete roof softened by the timber screen draws its inspiration from the local architecture's unique hybrid of mass and lightweight elements.

Opposite top right and opposite bottom A series of courtyards, gardens and other planted terraces is deftly woven throughout the architecture, combining structured and naturalistic planting and creating a sense that the landscape and architecture are meaningfully integrated.

Above Site plan

Right Upper ground floor

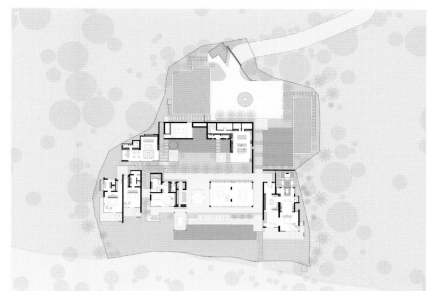

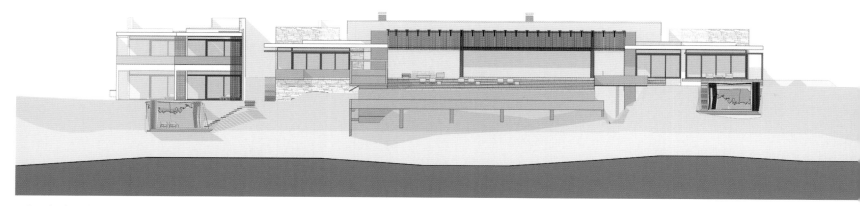

South elevation

Below, clockwise from left Layering of ceiling soffits: wood slats, plastered concrete, rough wood off-shutter concrete • Rough wood off-shutter concrete • Angled and overlapping copper screen • Punctured skylights of kitchen pavilion • Local hand-chiselled black andesite stone walls • Locally sourced teak sun screens

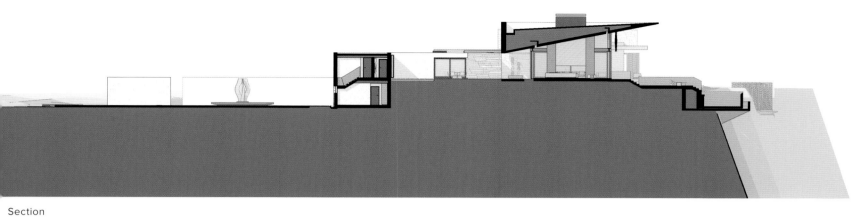

Section

Opposite Local stone is overlaid with distinctive timberwork to create texture.

Right The outdoor shower has local black andesite stone finishes.

Following spread The pool steps down from the main living terrace and becomes an extension of the ocean.

BORA

Mallorca   Spain

This relaxed resort-style home and work environment on the island of Mallorca, Spain, is a short flight from the client's native Germany. Blending into its surrounding bucolic landscape through its use of form and locally inspired materials, it reflects a contemporary take on Mallorca's architecture. The client's vision for Bora was inspired by the airy light-filled spaces of SAOTA's Cape Town projects that they had previously visited.

The complex, steeply sloping site required careful placement of the building to provide comfortable pedestrian and vehicular access. Its length allowed for the creation of a linear terraced building with every important room, on both the terrace and bedroom level, having uninterrupted views, with an emphasis on outdoor living.

The linear arrangement is interspersed with green pause spaces on both levels. Stone walls act as holding elements at the ends of the building. The three bedroom blocks on the upper level are separated with lush courtyards all tied together by the steel holding edge beams. The building is a fusion of a contemporary approach with regional influences. The traditional curved-tile roofs in the area inspired the exterior upper eaves and the internal gallery, where the forms are reinterpreted as a series of stone vaults.

The building's materials are layered, including plaster, stone, wooden pergolas and shutters, aluminium and large expanses of glass. The entry forecourt leads into the main living level, which opens on to a shaded outdoor terrace, raised half a level above the pool. Internally the space is arranged as a series of individual open-plan areas. There is a seamless flow between indoors and outdoors. The pergolas and tree canopies control the sunlight and create a gentle dappled interior feel. On the upper level, bedrooms open into a light-filled gallery with the signature barrel-vaulted ceilings, echoed from the exterior.

The building reflects a passive design approach, with deep overhangs, sliding shutters, screens and recessed doors and windows, with natural light and ventilation flooding the interior spaces. The interiors, by ARRCC and RyS Arquitectos, are neutral and understated, with accents of textured and hand-crafted pieces. The brief was to create a balance between comfort and elegance.

Architect of record: RyS Arquitectos

Opposite Inspired by the vernacular architecture of Mallorca, the house is composed of cubic white forms terraced down the landscape. The local 'Spanish' tile roofs have been reinterpreted in sandstone curved panels in the roof.

Following spread Exterior walls are from natural limestone. The length of the site allowed for the creation of a linear terraced building.

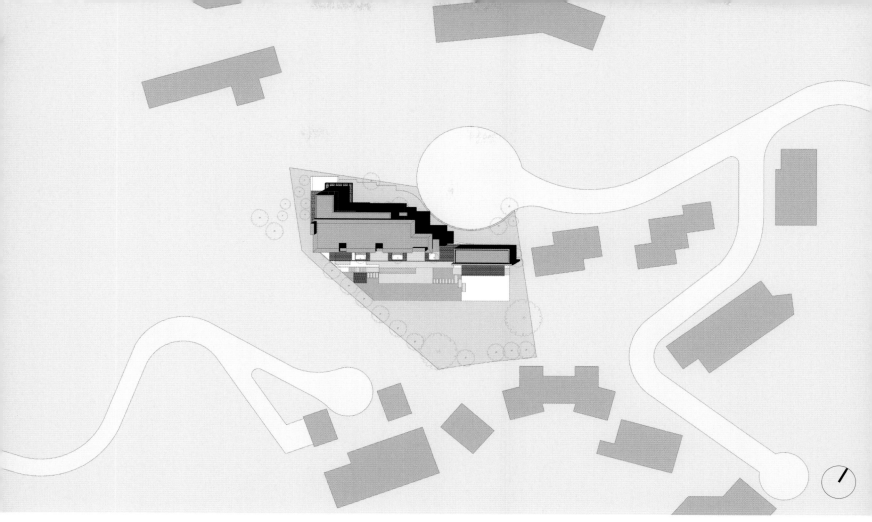

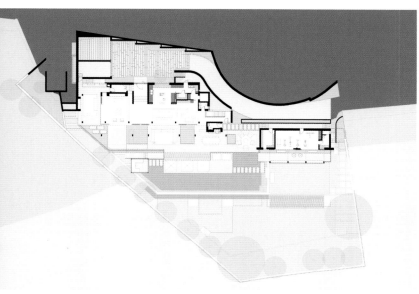

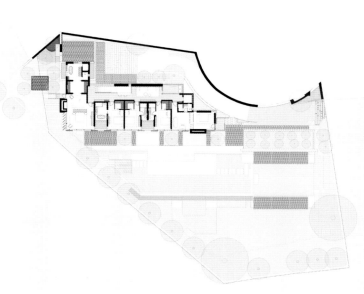

Opposite top The main living level blends seamlessly with the outdoor terrace, which is sheltered by pergolas that create soft dappled light.

Opposite bottom The interiors were designed to be neutral, with soft layers that complement the stone and natural elements included in the exterior. Artworks are by Marco Grassi and part of the homeowner's private collection.

Top Site plan

Above left Ground floor

Above right First floor

0   10   20m
0   20   40   60ft

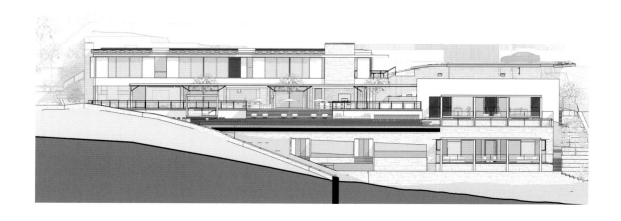

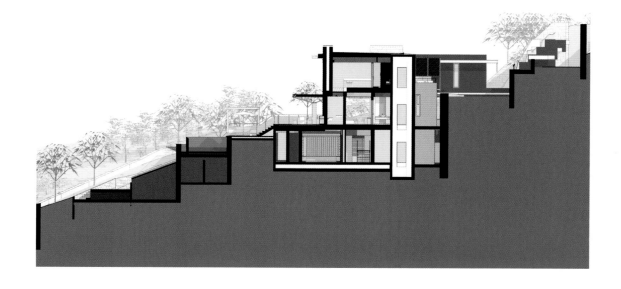

Above right South elevation

Right Section

Opposite, clockwise from top left Exterior travertine eaves reinterpreted as a series of stone vaults • Mild-steel-framed pivoting shutters with timber infills • Interior timber screening • Pergolas and tree canopies to control the sunlight • Travertine barrel-vaulted ceilings • Shadows of timber screens on timber garage doors

Opposite Mild-steel-framed pivoting shutters with timber infills create privacy.

Right Travertine barrel-vaulted ceilings are reinterpreted from exterior upper eaves. The artwork is by Marco Grassi.

Following spread Stone walls act as holding elements at the ends of the building.

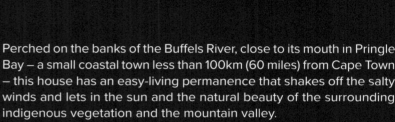

RESTIO RIVER

Pringle Bay South Africa

Perched on the banks of the Buffels River, close to its mouth in Pringle Bay – a small coastal town less than 100km (60 miles) from Cape Town – this house has an easy-living permanence that shakes off the salty winds and lets in the sun and the natural beauty of the surrounding indigenous vegetation and the mountain valley.

The architecture is clean and robust. It has a gravitas to it The materials are hard-wearing and resistant to the tough coastal climate and its winds that periodically sweep the bay.

The individual open-plan rooms flow seamlessly, forming one extended living zone and central space. The welcoming kitchen and lounge area is at the centre, with a sofa in the kitchen large enough to seat the entire family. The living rooms have a direct relationship with one another and the flow between these spaces adds a unique dynamic to the house.

The house faces due north, with a large stairwell that floods morning light into the kitchen area. The westerly façades of lounge and terrace look towards Cape Point, the most southerly tip of Cape Town's False Bay.

The character and interior architecture of the kitchen area demonstrate a fresh approach to living. With the addition of some custom-made pieces from ARRCC – including the sofas and dining table in neutral tones – the house is geared to the enjoyment of weekends away. Shades of white and grey fabrics are accented with original Moroccan Berber rugs and colourful kilims, complemented with solid French oak coffee tables and lacquered round timber stools. The use of soft leathers, white linens and rich textures creates an immediate sense of calm.

A warm, playful and quirky element to the home is added with the punched brass cladding to the lounge fireplace as well as the graphic lighting installation from Flos. The dining room features a custom-made table by James Mudge that is accentuated by the Lindsey Adelman pendant light. The black Magis chairs are softened with sheepskin throws.

The property being situated at good elevation with lots of access to the surrounding fynbos (scrubland), the natural choice for landscaping was to incorporate as much indigenous vegetation as possible around the house and in the internal courtyard. The addition of three typical South African trees – milkwood, coral trees and waterberries – make this an iconic South African family holiday home.

Opposite The main bedroom upstairs boasts panoramic views of the mountain and valley.

Following spread The covered outdoor terrace allows for seamless indoor–outdoor transitions.

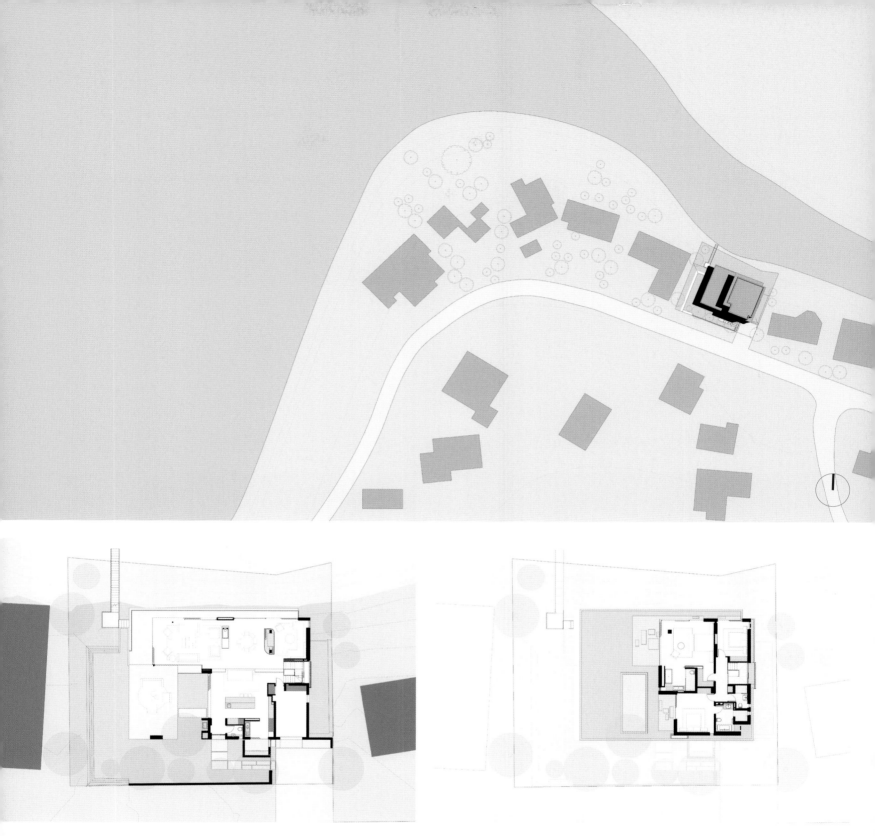

Opposite top The view from the first floor to the terrace below reveals the spatial relationship between levels, which allows for vertical connections and lines of sight, particularly via the cut-out above the courtyard.

Opposite bottom The main bedroom boasts panoramic views of the mountain and valley. The neutral colour palette and modest furniture pieces of the bedrooms allow the incredible views to be the focus like ever-changing artworks.

Top Site plan

Above left Ground floor

Above right First floor

0   5   10m
0   10   20   30ft

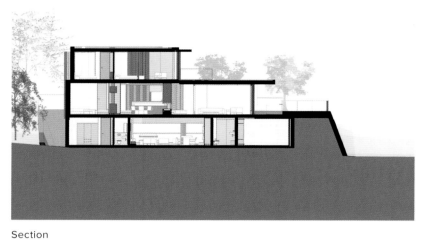

Section

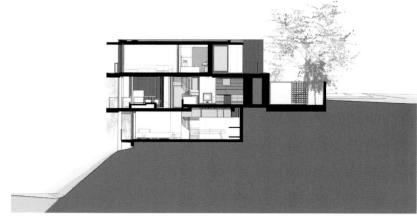

Section

Below, clockwise from top left Steel staircase with bagged and painted brick screen walls • Mild-steel spiral staircase from below • Painted vertical timber slat cladding with terrazzo ledges • Aluminium cladding to upper level and concrete roof edge • Granite stone chips to flat roofs • Punched brass cladding of lounge fireplace • Painted vertical timber slat cladding with terrazzo floors and ledges

North elevation

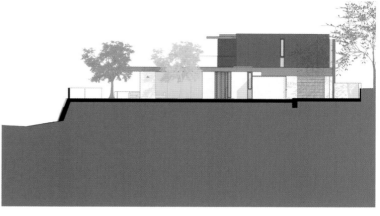

South elevation

Opposite The central dining space includes a feature light and an open fireplace of punched brass cladding. The black Magis chairs are softened with sheepskin throws.

Right The bathroom has vertical timber cladding and a terrazzo floor.

Following spread The extended living zone forms a largely fluid space, with areas subtly differentiated without being divided. Custom-made sofas in the lounge area are covered in white fabric, brightened with Berber rugs and kilims. The vast windows look out towards Cape Point, the most southerly tip of Cape Town's False Bay, offering sunset views.

LA LUCIA
Durban   South Africa

This beach house in La Lucia on the north coast of KwaZulu-Natal province was designed to create relaxed, uncomplicated but luxurious spaces for its owners. The property enjoys direct sea-facing frontage with fantastic ocean views and includes several magnificent protected milkwood trees. While the site offers a wonderful sense of connection to the surrounding dunes and natural coastal vegetation, it is sometimes battered by the north-easterly winds and storms.

The double-storey house maximizes the views across the beach and sea while seamlessly integrating the ground level with the external terraces, pool decks and landscaping. It has been sensitively nestled among the milkwood trees, two of which flank the relatively austere entrance, taking centre stage until the cinematic panorama is revealed from the double-volume hallway.

All the living spaces on the ground level open either on to the sea-facing pool deck to the east or on to the garden to the west, which is beautifully lit by afternoon sun. The open-plan living space can be enjoyed as a single continuous span or arranged to create separately defined areas. The terrace, swimming pool and deck are slightly elevated to provide views over the dune plants and to reinforce the connection with the ocean. On the upper level, each of the four sea-facing bedrooms has its own private terrace.

The eastern façade has been 'wrapped' with a series of bronzed anodized-aluminium sliding screens, which can be used to close off the interior and terrace entirely or in part. The screens are perforated with a graphic representation of a milkwood tree, which reveals itself once they are fully closed. From the outside, this image creates the home's identity, and from the inside it resembles a view through branches, further integrating the house with its surroundings.

An internal courtyard between the braai area and external dining terrace brings the landscaping to the edge of the living areas, breaking the expanse of the external terrace and also reinforcing the connection between interior and exterior. It becomes the lush green heart of the building, softening the architecture and creating visual interest.

The materials selected for the external spaces echo bleached driftwood and the beach: weathered iroko, honed sandstone and sand-coloured polished concrete floors. The concrete floors continue inside, complemented with bleached timber. The ceilings are clad with aligned timber slats that draw the eye towards the seascape.

Opposite At night the screens on the eastern façade appear translucent, highlighting the milkwood tree graphic.

Following spread The strong linearity of the beach-facing pool terrace elevation is softened by the sliding shutters.

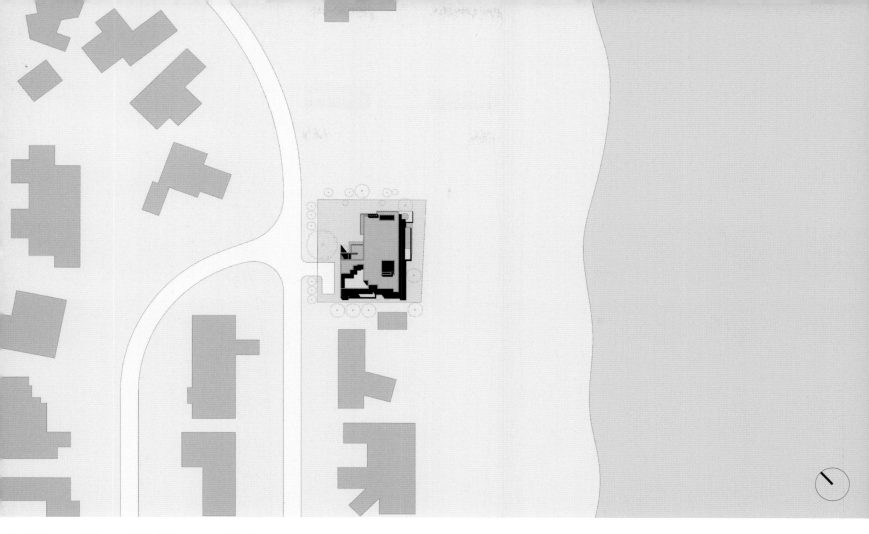

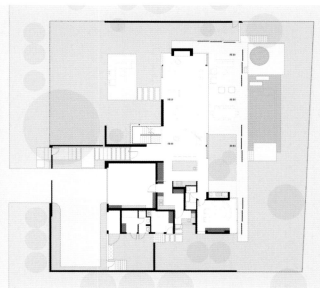

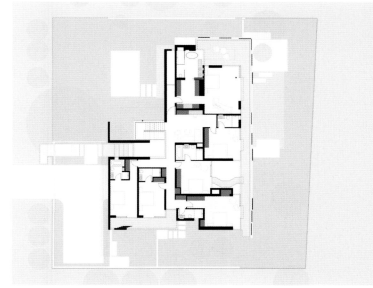

Opposite top From the rear garden, a fully glazed staircase can be seen leading to the upper level of the home. This secondary courtyard space provides a protected private sanctuary, away from the ocean and prevailing winds, with landscaping designed to enclose and define the space, creating an external room as an extension of the home's living areas.

Opposite bottom The master bathroom has a sandblasted shower screen and sandstone-clad wall. Also visible are the bronzed anodized-aluminium sliding screens, which can be used to close off the interior and terrace entirely or in part.

Top Site plan

Above left Ground floor

Above right First floor

0		5		10m
0	10	20		30ft

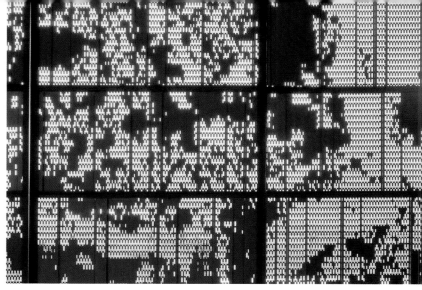

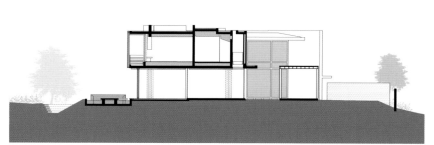

Section

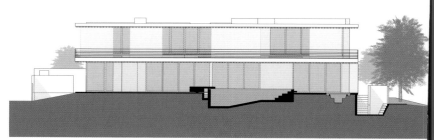

South-east elevation

Above, clockwise from left Milkwood trees, inspiration for façade screens • Patterned screens mimicking the milkwood trees • Floating timber staircase • Bronzed anodized-aluminium sliding screens • Veined white marble main bedroom fireplace • Timber slats fixed to the off-shutter soffit • Timber slats fixed to the off-shutter soffit • Bronzed anodized-aluminium sliding screens

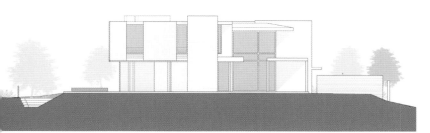
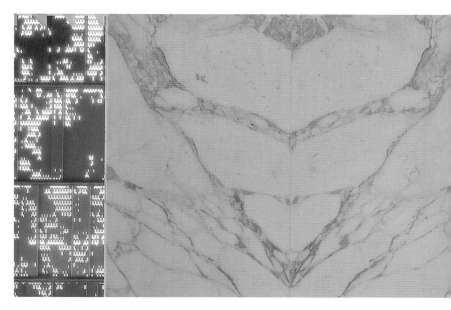

North-east elevation

North-west elevation

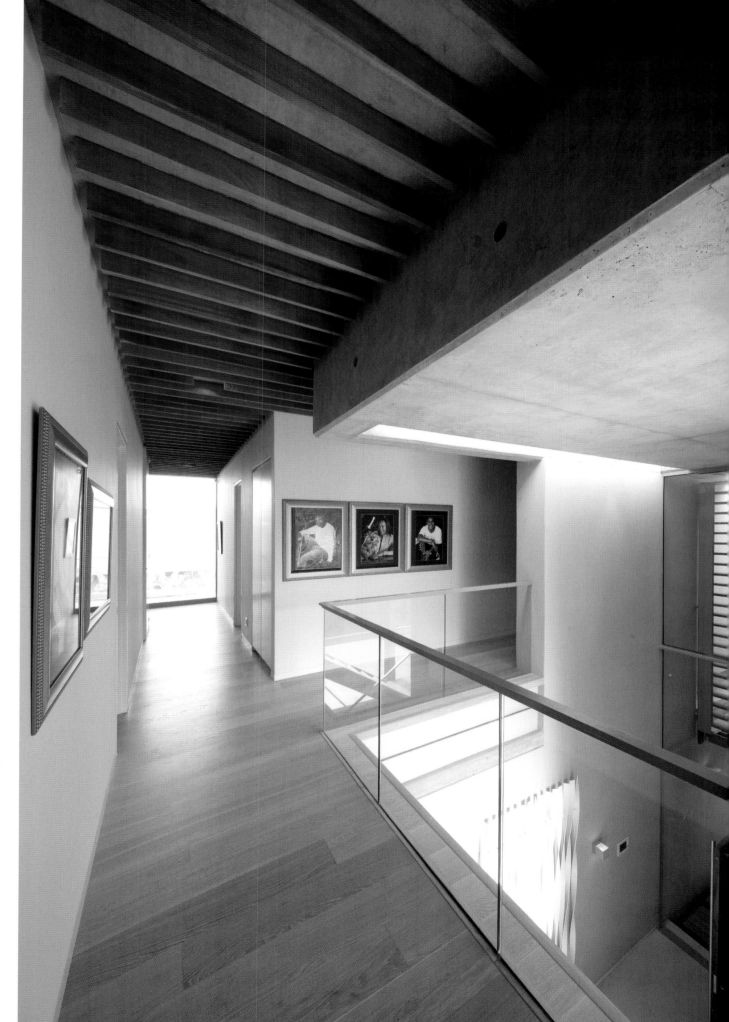

Opposite A floating timber step platform and pergola lead towards the entrance of the home as a milkwood tree welcomes guests.

Right View from the upper-level passage: a double-volume entrance area provides a light well and acts as a linking element between levels.

Following spread Bronze aluminium sliding screens envelop internal living spaces.

BEACHY HEAD

Plettenberg Bay   South Africa

This family holiday home in Plettenberg Bay in South Africa's Western Cape province is situated on a dune that slopes down to the beach and has uninterrupted views over the Indian Ocean, Robberg and the Outeniqua Mountains. The brief called for an elegant, relaxing home that could comfortably accommodate large-scale entertaining and yet feel intimate and cosy when the owners visited alone.

The house was conceived as a simple textured concrete box floating over the dune, capturing and framing the views. Seen from the beach, the building is expressed as a stone plinth with bedrooms above it. From the street, the scale of the house appears modest, the living spaces concealed on the lower level.

To exploit the maximum permitted height, the sculptural southern part of the upper level is raised and appears sliced off from the northern part by a vertical opening that extends through the building, washing northern light deep into the interiors. Lit from a skylight above, the stairs are delicately suspended in this void, allowing views into the column-free living area. The bedroom wing above is supported by a large sculptural fireplace lined with woven oxidized copper salvaged from discarded hot-water cylinders. The geometry of the staircase continues as a diagonal line that extends the cantilevering entertainment terrace towards Robberg.

Large sliders permit unhindered access between the wind-protected entertainment courtyard, the living space and the front terrace. The kitchen is positioned to serve the living spaces and the northern courtyard and opens upwards, connecting with the gallery passage above and allowing in natural light.

Large timber sliding shutters protect the bedrooms from the morning light and ensure privacy. The main bedroom is on the higher part of the upper level to take advantage of the ocean views. Raised en-suite bathrooms allow unobstructed views from all bedrooms and bathrooms. Large mirrors at the ends of the rooms accentuate the space and reflect views.

The lower level accommodates a games room, guest suite, audio-visual room and services. The pool, which is also on this level, connects to the main entertainment spaces via a stone staircase, articulated as part of the plinth. The pool is situated centrally on the terrace to allow the main tanning deck to extend to the end of the site to catch the afternoon sun. A firepit in the far corner, close to the beach, is protected from the wind by glass panels.

The water level of the rim-flow pool protrudes 20mm (¾in) above the timber deck, creating the impression that the water body slots into it, further unifying this refined home and its natural surroundings.

Opposite Two floating boxes hover over the fynbos (scrubland) dunes, blending in with the surrounding environment.

Following spread View from the road: a strong horizontal entrance canopy is planted with indigenous shrubs.

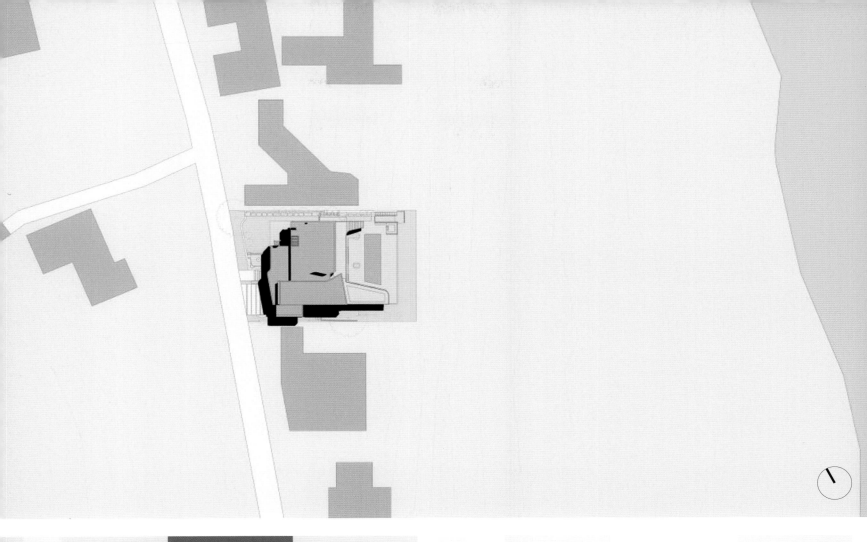

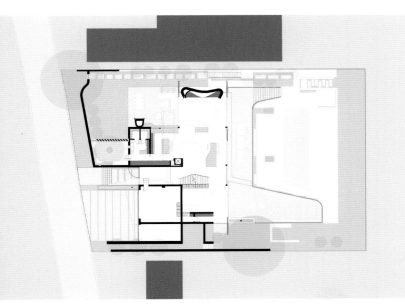

Opposite top In the north courtyard a pizza oven chimney is a strong vertical element, counterbalancing the horizontal entrance canopy and floating bedroom wing.

Opposite bottom The staircase is delicately suspended within a carved vertical opening, allowing views through it and lit from a skylight above. The opening brings northern light into the deeper interior spaces of the house.

Top Site plan

Above left Ground floor

Above right First floor

```
0        5      10m
0    10    20   30ft
```

East elevation

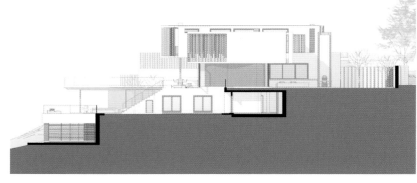

North elevation

Below, clockwise from left Stained oak irregular bathroom screen • Grey sandstone wall cladding • Resin-stucco polished curvilinear plaster wall • Grey sandstone wall cladding • Terrazzo tiles around infinity edge of pool • Vertical timber screen façade for shading and privacy • Suspended staircase within roof-lit carved opening

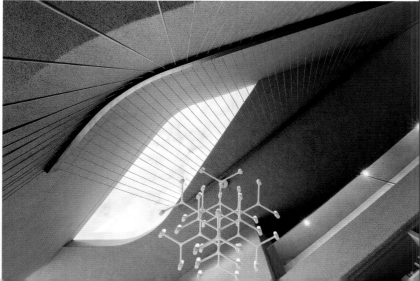

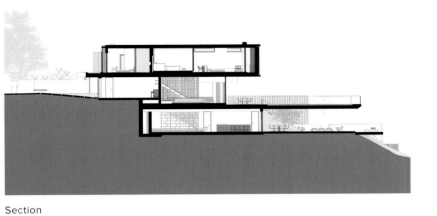

Section

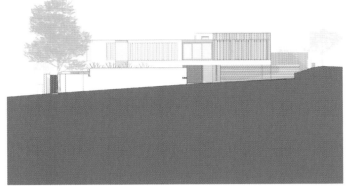

West elevation

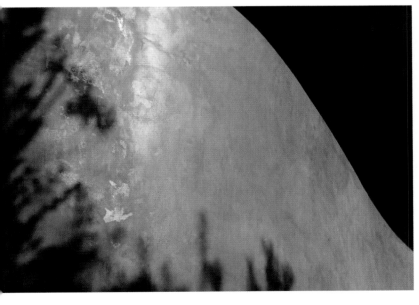

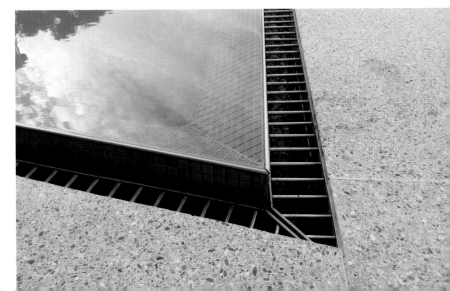

Left The carved opening in which the staircase is suspended not only lets in natural light from a skylight above it, but also opens up views towards the front terrace and the beach.

Opposite top The cantilevered terrace allows uninterrupted views. Timber shutters protect the façade from the morning sun.

Oppposite bottom The suspended staircase acts as a partition between the dining and lounge areas.

Following spread The pool is located on the lower terrace but remains connected to the main entertainment spaces via a stone staircase.

Pages 164–65 Lion's Head and the Twelve Apostles, Cape Town, South Africa.

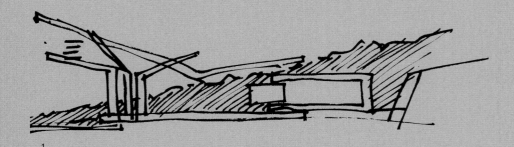

1

2

3

4

PATRONS

Stefan Antoni

Architecture, by its nature, is dependent on the support of patrons. Clients with courage, vision and resources have initiated and sustained the work of architects throughout history. I.M. Pei spent the first decade of his career working mainly for a single client, New York real-estate developer William Zeckendorf, who hired him soon after graduating. The body of work that Pei designed for Zeckendorf was the springboard to an illustrious career that gave us many important buildings, such as the Louvre Pyramid. In South Africa, the pioneering modernist Gawie Fagan built his career designing more than fifty banks for Volskas Bank.

Senegalese businessman Yerim Sow has played this role for SAOTA. Sow is a serial entrepreneur, who built his fortune in telecoms in West Africa and whose passion for architecture has resulted in repeat commissions for SAOTA and some of our best buildings.

I first met Yerim in 2000. He had just bought an apartment in Granger Bay on the Victoria and Albert Waterfront in Cape Town and needed an architect to turn it into something special. En route to the airport, he stopped to meet me. His brief was simple: 'Do something *magique* and tell me when it's finished.' He paid the fee the following day, and we set about tackling the commission. Some months later, we informed Yerim, by fax, that the project was complete. He was delighted with the result, and the next project for him was a luxury hotel in Dakar, Senegal. Twenty-one years and more than forty projects later, we are still working together, the unwritten rule being, 'Don't show me anything boring!' The excitement generated by each commission sets the stage for the next one, often in challenging and uncompromising locations.

Lake House, one of his developments located in Geneva, is featured in this book (see page 250). We have designed apartments, offices, houses, hotels, wine estates and resorts for him in Dakar, Cape Town, Conakry, Barcelona, Geneva, Abidjan, Douala and Paris; the list seems endless.

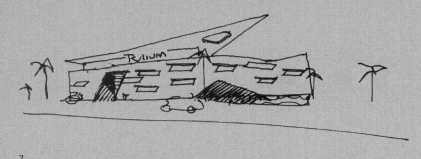

7

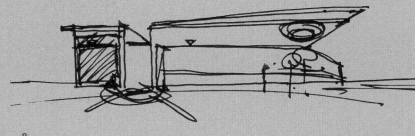

8

9

Hats off to Yerim for persevering with his architectural ambition, often against substantial odds, completing pioneering projects and setting new standards, each eagerly emulated by his competitors.

Many of our clients become friends. The practice of architecture is challenging and demanding, and the friendships are a testament to a shared vision and a belief in the transformational power of architecture.

Figs 1, 2 Popenguine, Dakar, Senegal; fig. 3 Cliff House, Dakar, Senegal; fig. 4 Granger Bay, Cape Town, South Africa; fig. 5 Stefan Antoni & Yerim Sow; fig. 6 Teyliom Tower, Dakar, Senegal; figs 7, 8, 9 THQ, Dakar, Senegal; figs 10, 11 CSE HQ, Dakar, Senegal; figs 12, 16 Dakar Mermoz, Dakar Senegal; fig. 13 Gymnasium, Dakar, Senegal; fig. 14 Hotel Conakry, Conakry, Guinea; fig. 15 Sushi Bar, Dakar, Senegal; fig. 17 The One, Dakar, Senegal; fig. 18 Barcelona Apartment, Spain; fig. 19 Paris Apartment, France; fig. 20 Sindia Camp, Sindia, Senegal; fig. 21 Noom La Reserve, Dakar, Senegal; figs 22, 25 Radisson Blu Hotel, Dakar, Senegal; fig. 23 Free HQ, Dakar, Senegal; fig. 24 Sindia Resort, Sindia, Senegal; fig. 26 DTS, Dakar, Senegal; fig. 27 Hotel Abidjan, Abidjan, Côte d'Ivoire; fig. 28 Hotel Cotonou, Cotonou, Benin; fig. 29 Cannebière, Abidjan, Côte d'Ivoire; fig. 30 Hotel Pointe-Noire, Pointe-Noire, Congo

10

11

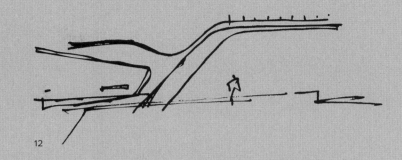

12

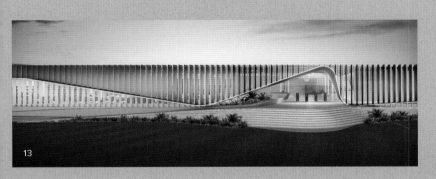

13

16

14

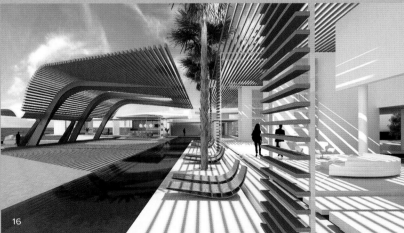

17

15

18

19

20

23

21

24

22

25

26

27

28

29

30

VENUS

Cape Town   South Africa

The Table Bay coastline north of Cape Town's city centre is renowned as much for its iconic views of Table Mountain as for being one of the world's top kitesurfing destinations. The beaches are beautiful, but the weather conditions can be harsh, with winds blowing in from multiple directions.

This dune-side holiday home, which has direct access to the beach, is designed as much to open up to the uninterrupted ocean views as it is to provide sheltered areas inside and out to enable a relaxing indoor–outdoor lifestyle.

A monolithic exterior addresses the public domain of the street, which gives way to an unfolding sequence of spaces, mediating a layered experience from the threshold towards a light, transparent front that frames panoramic views.

The courtyard between the off-street entrance and the living pavilion creates a transitional outdoor space, at the same time allowing the living pavilion to be transparent on both sides. A patio and swimming pool extend into the courtyard behind the living pavilion, where it is sheltered on all four sides from the wind.

The horizontal emphasis of the design takes its cue not only from the wide dunes and horizons, but also from the vast cargo ships that cross Table Bay. Two curvaceous copper-clad towers anchor the building on each side, contrasting with the low-slung character of the house while providing practical functions such as vertical circulation.

Copper was chosen partly because of the verdigris that develops on it over time, which complements the grey-green dune vegetation and also expresses the effects of the maritime climate in its robust but naturally weathered appearance, reminiscent of the ever-present cargo ships.

As such, it is quite distinct from SAOTA's work on the Atlantic seaboard, which tends to respond more emphatically to the powerful natural presences of Table Mountain and the ocean, whereas this coastline offers a perspective of the mercantile dimension of the city. It is this expressly manmade quality, however, that allows the house to appear so distinctly of its place, just as a hulk or shipwreck is clearly engineered but has an undercurrent of transience, almost as if it were being reclaimed by nature.

The view of Table Mountain, at 45 degrees to the left of the dominant sea-facing view, brings complexity to the spatial experience of the interiors by introducing implied diagonal lines within the extended linearity of the floorplan. Perhaps most fundamental to the experience of this beach house, however, is its sense of itself as part of a dynamic spatial and temporal continuum, mediating an ever-changing relationship with the landscape and climate.

Opposite The stairwell in the entrance fits into one of the curvaceous copper-clad towers on the right-hand side of the home as you walk through the entrance. The sculpture is by Dylan Lewis.

Following spread The courtyard creates a transitional outdoor space in the progression from street to beachfront, and also allows the living pavilion to be transparent on both sides, emphasizing a sense of continuity.

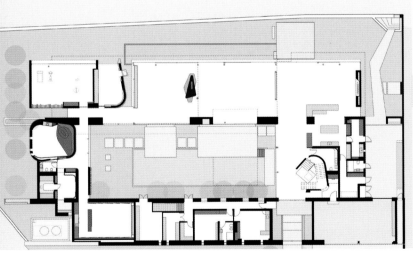

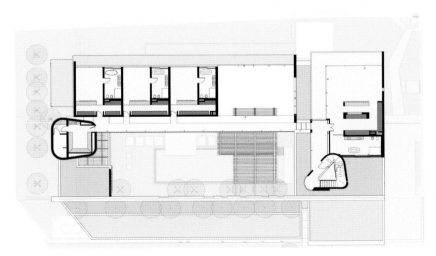

Opposite top From the beach, the horizontal emphasis of the design takes its cue from the sand dunes and wide horizons.

Opposite bottom The timber pergola in the courtyard extends into the interior, blurring the distinction between inside and outside.

Top Site plan

Above left Ground floor

Above right First floor

```
0        5      10m
0    10    20    30ft
```

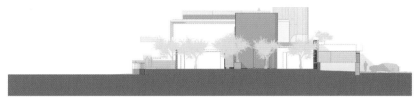

South elevation

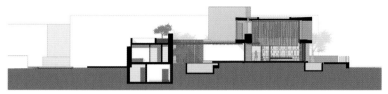

Section

Below, clockwise from left Entrance foyer water feature in Wild Sea granite • Roof timber in oak • Guest bathroom with marble splashback • Bespoke door handle to spa bathroom based on architectural curves of staircase • Floors and stairs in Magic Grey granite with New Rustenburg granite inlays • Bespoke oxidized copper door handle to spa based on architectural curves of staircase • Stairwell walls clad in oxidized copper

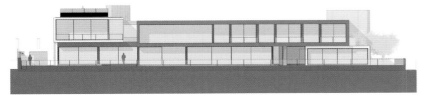

West elevation

Section

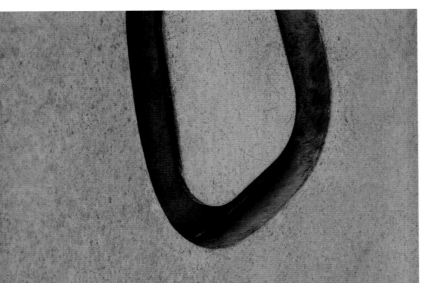

Left The interior design responds in many ways to the architectural envelope. Its contemporary, luxurious but leisurely approach sought to incorporate an overt emphasis on collaborations with local artists and designers, to express a distinct sense of place.

Opposite top The combinations of refined and raw materiality in the architecture are sustained in the interiors. In key areas, such as the stairwell, the copper cladding of the towers is carried through into the interior.

Opposite bottom The patio and pool extend into a garden courtyard behind the living pavilion, where it is sheltered on all four sides.

Following spread Table Mountain is visible from the living areas at a diagonal to the main sea-facing view, cutting across the linearity of the space.

DI LIDO

Miami   USA

The setting for this Miami house on a pie-shaped lot on the southern tip of Di Lido Island offers views of the islands, downtown and South Beach. The house spills out on to a long waterfront elevation to evoke the experience of being on the deck of a superyacht. The harmonious merging of internal and external living spaces that characterizes this terrace is sustained throughout the house.

Entrance from the street, via the Venetian Causeway, which crosses Biscayne Bay between Miami and Miami Beach, is restrained; lush planting skirts an in–out driveway, and a series of wall planes and volumes, held together by a curved screen of etched glass, signals a double-volume entrance hall. Once inside, the programme pulls apart to form a dramatic canyon that frames the view. This central void is animated with sculptural elements and artworks, including a spiral staircase and a series of bronze screens that hang from the ceiling and create a double-height dining room separate from the kitchen and family space.

All the principal living spaces – from the intimate areas housing a kitchen, butler kitchen and family den to the expansive great room and study – give out on to a collection of semi-covered external living rooms rimmed by the arc of the bayside. Water features meander throughout the house, from a pond at the entrance to a calm reflection pool around the study, unifying the lido-like outdoor area while creating smaller islands of space and linking the interiors to the pool and the sea. The covered external living areas flow on to a spacious deck with lounging areas, deckchairs for sunbathing, shallow-water 'martini' seating, a bar and a pop-up outdoor table on the water's edge. With two mooring docks, the flow between land and sea is seamless.

A balance between scale and intimacy was achieved by composing the programme both between the wings on either side of the core and across the upper and lower floors. The upper bedroom level houses the sea-facing main suite and three on-the-water suites. This level hovers between the masses of the living level and a pre-oxidized copper roof, which, in a nod to the surrounding early 20th-century Italianate vernacular, traces a raked silhouette from crisp edge to sharp pitch. Here, a rooftop terrace – accessed by lift – includes a bar, a firepit and a hot tub with views of downtown Miami.

Crisp white stucco, warm grey limestone, and copper and bronze detail elements combine to suggest understated luxury and textural tension. This domestic palette is offset against cobalt-blue pools and lush, vivid green landscapes, resulting in a grounded, sophisticated and relaxed aesthetic.

Architect of record: KKAID

Opposite The tropical climate resulted in deep covered outdoor spaces and internal courtyards with landscaping endemic to Miami.

Following spread The entrance from the street is characterized by a series of wall planes held together by a curved screen of etched glass.

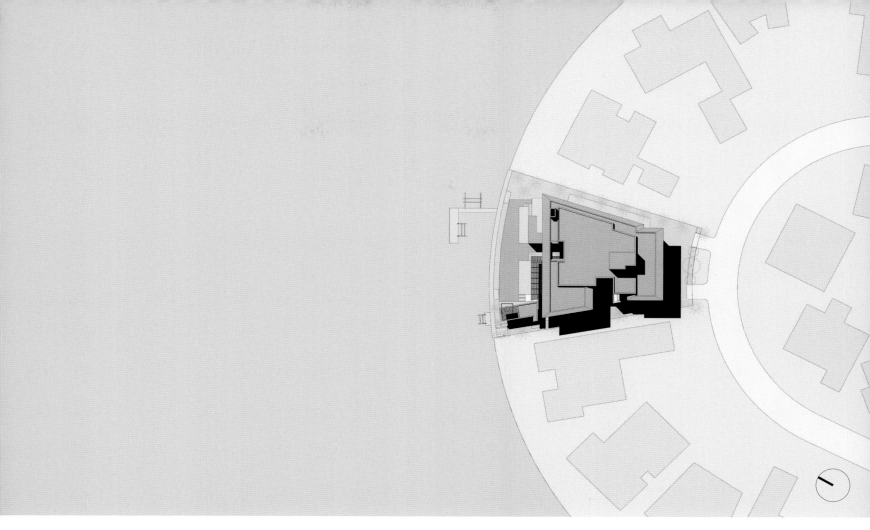

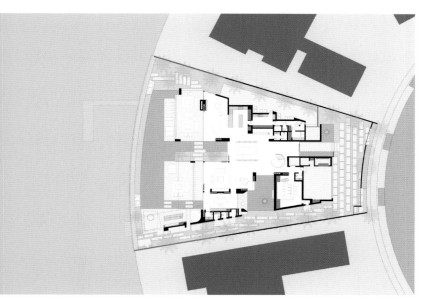

Opposite top The cobalt-blue pool and vivid green planting combine with the white stucco and grey limestone to produce a sophisticated and relaxed aesthetic on the edge of Biscayne Bay.

Opposite bottom Reflecting the setting of sea and islands, water is a feature throughout the house, from ponds to a reflection pool.

Top Site plan

Above left Ground floor

Above right First floor

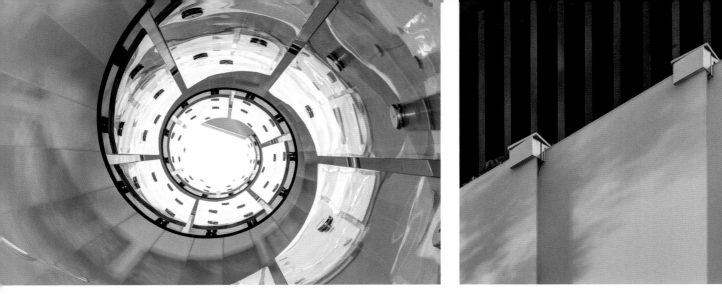

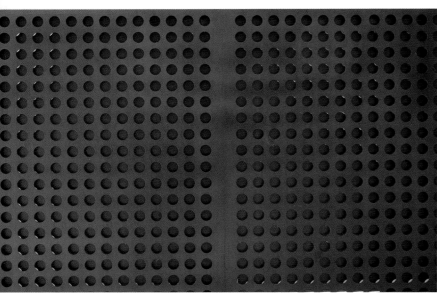

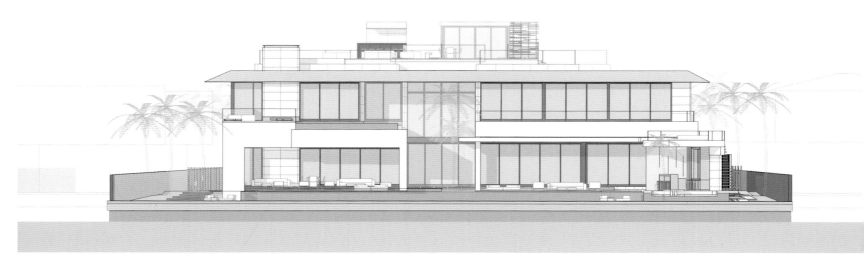

South elevation

Above, clockwise from top left Floating glass staircase
• Etched-glass curved entrance screen • Limestone walls
• Detail of suspended bronze double-volume dining room
screens • Suspended bronze double-volume dining room
screens • Aged copper ceiling soffits • Bronze-coloured
anodized-aluminium entrance gate

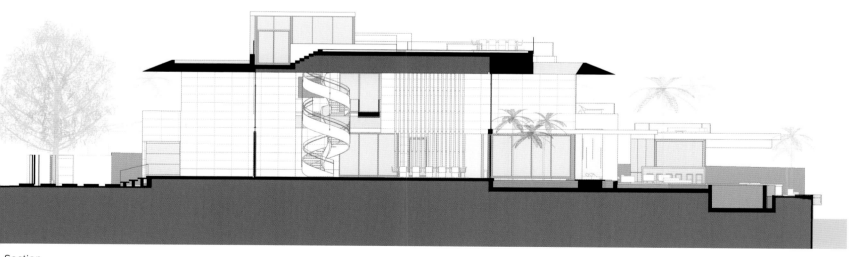

Section

Opposite top
The double-volume central void is animated by a dramatic spiral staircase and a series of sculptural suspended bronze screens that separate the kitchen and informal areas from the dining area.

Opposite bottom
The water feature at the double-volume entrance to the house wraps around and extends all the way to the front pool.

Right The void that runs through the centre of the living areas continues between the outdoor lounging areas, covered with a pre-oxidized copper roof that references some of the nearby Italianate vernacular dating back to the early 20th century.

Following spread Deep covered outdoor spaces create a seamless transition between land and water.

TERRACINA

Miami   USA

The character of this four-bedroom family home in Miami, Florida, arose largely through an engaged creative response to its distinctive setting. The house is located on a wedge-shaped lot in the city of Golden Beach, a small municipality on a narrow strip of land between the Atlantic Ocean on the east and the Intracoastal Waterway to the west.

The site, at the end of a cul-de-sac, features spectacular views up the wide span of the Intracoastal Waterway to the north-west and unusually extensive water frontage along its radius edge. The house has been positioned near to the boundary line towards the back of the property to maximize waterside frontage.

SAOTA adopted a layered approach in which the house mediates a progressive experience that unfolds between a muscular, monolithic protective screen of concrete panels presented to the street and a light, transparent treatment on the façade facing the waterway. The transition from its bold public presence on the street through the gallery-like interior (offering tantalizing glimpses of the water beyond) is intensified by the weighty threshold. The internal spaces then advance by degrees towards the external spaces, becoming lighter as the architecture opens towards the view. This experience extends all the way to a cantilevered deck at the water's edge that facilitates boat access.

A spine along the eastern property line accommodates a kitchen and back-of-house functions, including a gym. From it, three 'fingers' stretch out at right angles in the direction of the waterway, accommodating the living rooms and a series of shaded terraces that peel away from the outlook. On the top level, the fingers accommodate bedrooms, which also step back so that each room upstairs has an uninterrupted view of the Intracoastal Waterway.

This fragmented scheme not only responds to the water's edge and the vistas beyond, but also breaks down the building mass, allowing the landscaping to interrupt the plan and natural light to flood into the rooms. This porous arrangement creates a rhythmic series of landscaped outdoor 'rooms' and covered outdoor terraces.

SAOTA's lifestyle-driven approach to contemporary design plays out not only in this home's engagement with its setting, but also through its tactile finishes. A simplified palette of materials including travertine, walnut and quartzite has been used consistently in warm tones throughout the entire home, grounding the architecture and enhancing the home's relationship with its setting by making it seem almost like an extension or extrapolation of its environment.

Architect of record: DVICE INC.

Opposite The bold, weighty façade presented to the arrival forecourt is tempered with the embracing landscaping

Following spread A long, narrow rim-flow lap pool is easily accessible from the outdoor terraces, while steps leading to a cantilevered deck at the water's edge facilitate boat access. The artwork is *Becky* (2017) by Boo Ritson.

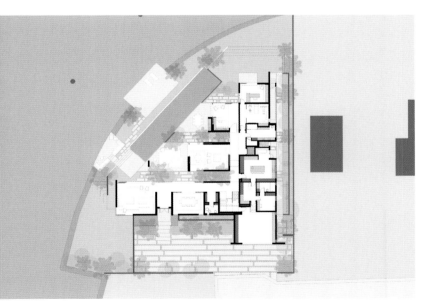

Opposite top Lush emerald plantings of broad-leaf Alocasia California and cascading railroad vine – including roof gardens – integrate the contemporary building with its setting.

Opposite bottom The lightness and delicacy of the interiors is articulated on the water-facing façade with a series of bead-blasted brassy laser-cut perforated aluminium screens, which contrast with a palette of stucco and unfilled travertine.

Top Site plan

Above left Ground floor

Above right First floor

0   5   10m
0   10   20   30ft

North elevation

South elevation

Above, clockwise from left Bead-blasted brassy laser-cut perforated aluminium screens on waterside façade • Monolithic protective screen of concrete panels • Unfilled travertine exterior walls • Walnut wood screen behind bath • Bead-blasted brassy laser-cut perforated aluminium screens • Cascading plantings of railroad vine • Staircase in travertine with walnut stair rails

Section

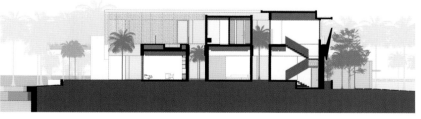
Section

Left The house presents itself to the street behind a monolithic protective screen of concrete panels.

Opposite top The interior architecture has been kept unfussy and simple to allow the owners' extensive collection of contemporary art full expression. The artwork here is by Richard Long (untitled).

Opposite bottom Covered terraces and outdoor rooms encourage the kind of indoor–outdoor relationship appropriate to Miami's waterside lifestyle and climate.

DOUBLE BAY
Sydney   Australia

Located in a north-facing cove in Sydney's vast natural harbour, the site of this family dwelling borders a park and a public pier that juts into the bay. This element forms one axis while a beach directly in front of the site forms another.

From the principal park elevation, the building appears as a collection of planes: a play on space, privacy and threshold. Graphite-coloured sail screens (made from polycarbonate chainmail developed for the *Lord of the Rings* films) provide privacy from the road. Timber cladding, plastered mass walls and a wood-clad soffit are layered into further planes, and the exaggerated sill of a bay window is punched through the sail screens, creating depth in an otherwise linear façade and providing privacy while maximizing light and views to the park.

Set into this façade, the stairwell is fully glazed but wrapped in a curved cloak of timber louvres, mediating the formal entrance and bedrooms above.

Entry is at 90 degrees to the bay, off the park. A ramp, edged by water, slopes gently up to the front door. Here the U-shaped plan of the house becomes clear. The entrance links the wings, separated by an internal garden, which allows views of the bay. Seen from the courtyard, the massive wall of the upper storey seems to weigh on the glazed lightness of the ground floor, amplifying the bay view.

The bayside wing of the house is a single open-plan space. Stairs rather than walls, differentiate the raised kitchen and family dining from the formal areas, extending seawards and drawing the eye towards the view while providing privacy. The garden is raised above the towpath for additional privacy from the beach.

An oversailing timber roof canopy is the home's defining motif. It connects the street side to the garden and the beach and permeates the interior, presenting itself at odd moments, protecting and defining both the internal and external spaces while expressing lightness, reflecting the sea and the canopies of the trees.

White walls and materials such as wood and travertine floors reflect the seaside setting. Accents of off-shutter concrete, like the rendered walls, appear soft and textured in contrast to the crisp screen and aluminium.

A playful character, the calculated blurring of boundaries and a fresh, layered composition cater to the domestic needs of a young family, while sharp lines, light forms and the lush integration of nature combine to make the design feel at home in its setting.

Architects in association: TKD Architects

Opposite Graphite-coloured polycarbonate chainmail sail screens are rigged off the house, providing privacy for the occupants.

Following spread From the street, the largely glazed lower storey is lost below crisp white walls, black-framed window boxes and sail screens.

MIKAYA

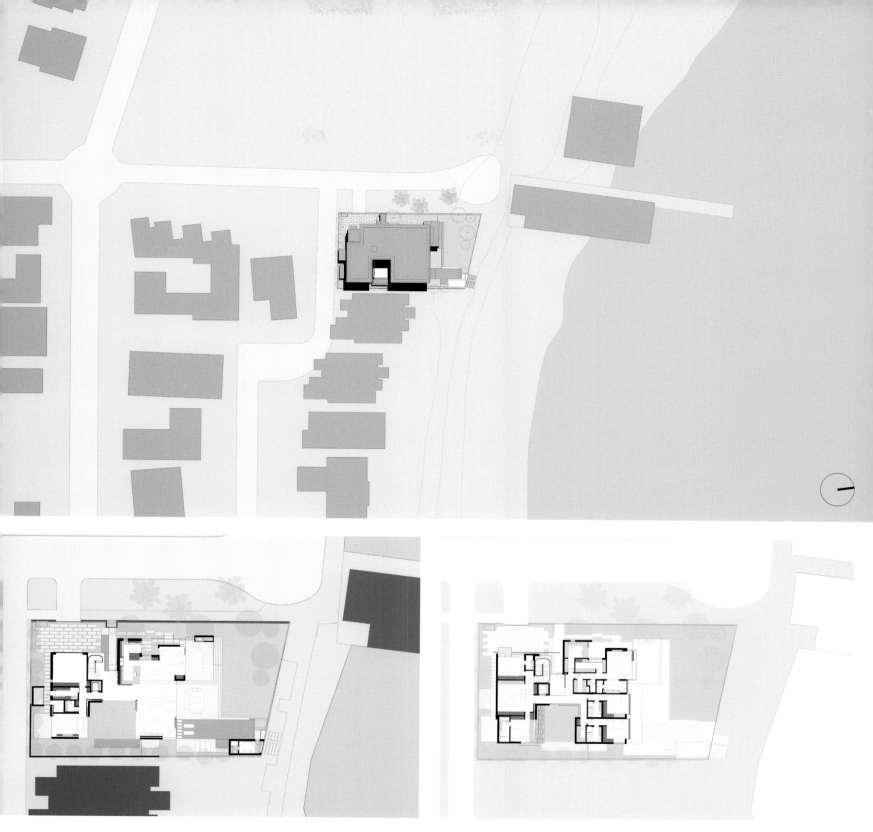

Opposite top The massive blank wall of the upper storey seems to weigh on the glazed lightness of the ground floor, amplifying the bay view visible from the internal courtyard garden.

Opposite bottom The bayside wing of the house is one open-plan space, with the kitchen and family dining raised to create a more informal area. The artwork is by Pae White.

Top Site plan

Above left Ground floor

Above right First floor

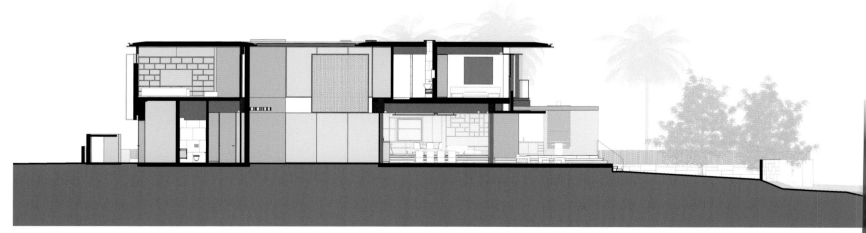

Section

Above, clockwise from left Staircase wrapped in a cloak of oak-veneer timber louvres with limewash finish • Polycarbonate chainmail sail screens • Honed white sandstone and powder-coated aluminium entrance gate • Oversailing Pacific teak timber battens on the ceiling soffit • Composition of timber cladding, plastered mass walls and wood-clad soffit • Polycarbonate chainmail sail screens providing privacy for top-level rooms • Detail of cloak of oak-veneer timber louvres of staircase

West elevation

Left The entrance, approached by a ramp, is a link between two wings separated by an internal garden, forming a U-shape.

Opposite The staircase in the fully glazed stairwell is wrapped in a cloak of oak-veneer timber louvres.

Following spread A horseshoe-shaped plan created a private internal courtyard that allowed landscaping and external areas to wrap around the key living spaces, maximizing light ingress, exposure to views and allowing spaces at the rear of the property to have views through the house to the harbour. The lower floor is completely glazed, with the more private spaces above enclosed within solid forms.

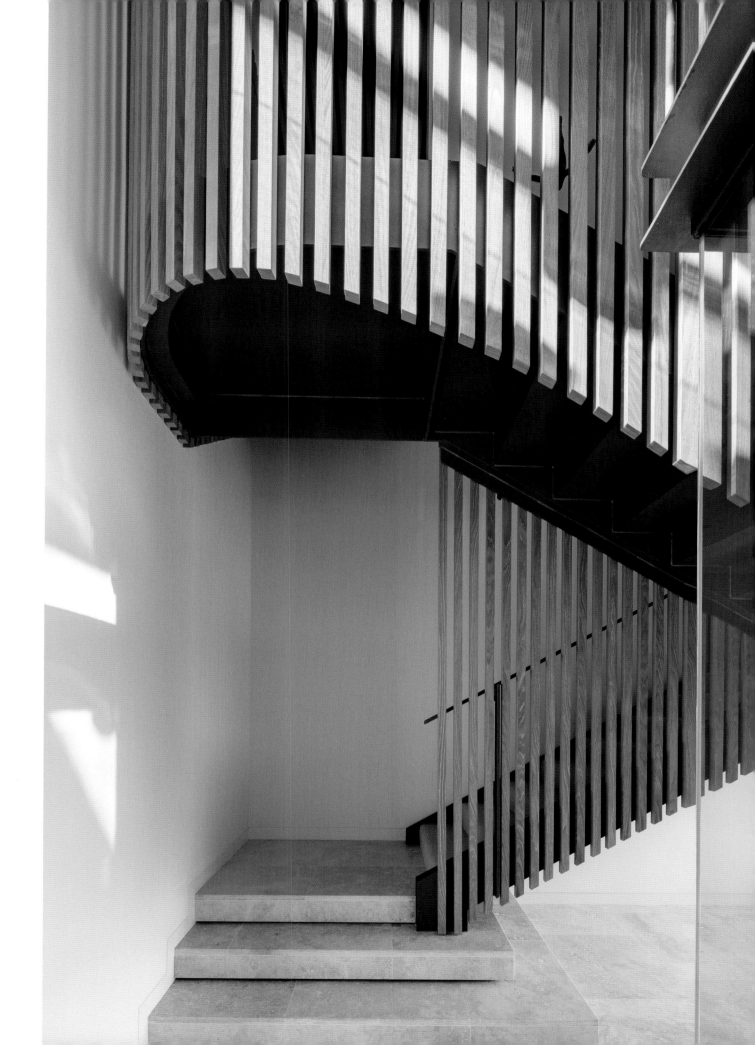

SILVER PINE
Moscow   Russia

In the Russian capital of Moscow, this contemporary home, set among the pinewoods on an island in the Moskva River, introduces a revolutionary outward-looking approach to the city's architectural tradition. This home represents the tradition of the terrace, with its emphasis on an outdoor orientation, but in a context and climate vastly different from the origin of the type. With modern glazing systems able to provide insulation in the Russian winter extremes, the real challenge was to mediate a dialogue between the two traditions to resolve the new approach harmoniously in the Russian context.

The pinewoods that the site overlooks are a significant motivation for the design's open, outward-facing orientation. This approach allowed SAOTA to explore an architecture that invites in natural light during the dark winter months to compensate for the lack of sun.

The architectural premise is one of contrasts: the street frontage's heavy protective presence speaks to the capital's monolithic architectural character, built to resist the extremes of heat and cold, which can vary by 40 degrees Celsius (70 degrees Fahrenheit) between seasons. Surrounding the main entrance is a sculptural buckle. This backlit, bronze-clad feature façade communicates the promise of the luxury and light interiors in the private spaces beyond the threshold and heightens the experience of crossing from the public realm to the private domain with its predominant treed landscape.

From the garden, the architecture presents a contrasting façade. Open fragmented glass walls invite views of the pines in, blurring the distinction between inside and outside. The outdoor terraces and the faceted, angular façade create courtyards and external rooms that facilitate an interaction between landscape and architecture that is a departure from the local tradition. In summer, it is possible to live outside as you might in South Africa or California. In winter, the interiors, which are nevertheless warm and cosy, can celebrate the beauty of the snowy landscape in a new approach to the harsh conditions, where the focus remains on the terrace rather than the hearth.

Silver-grey metal cladding on the exterior complements and enhances the green of the surrounding forest, providing an immersive landscape experience. Inside, natural materials predominate, from exotic marbles, some backlit, to metal and timber surfaces. Softer, warmer materials prevail upstairs, where the open, flowing and interconnected spatial approach gives way to private spaces with a more relaxed, casual atmosphere.

This project between SAOTA, ARRCC and Max Kasymov is the first completed SAOTA project in Russia. ARRCC proposed the concept idea for the interiors, and Max Kasymov, Moscow interior design studio, developed the project further and oversaw its realization.

Opposite The bronze-clad feature façade acts as a visual prompt towards the entrance opening on the otherwise relatively featureless façade.

Following spread The façade takes on the character of a natural material itself, highlighting a bespoke crafted quality in its detailing that speaks to the unique tailor-made approach to the house's design.

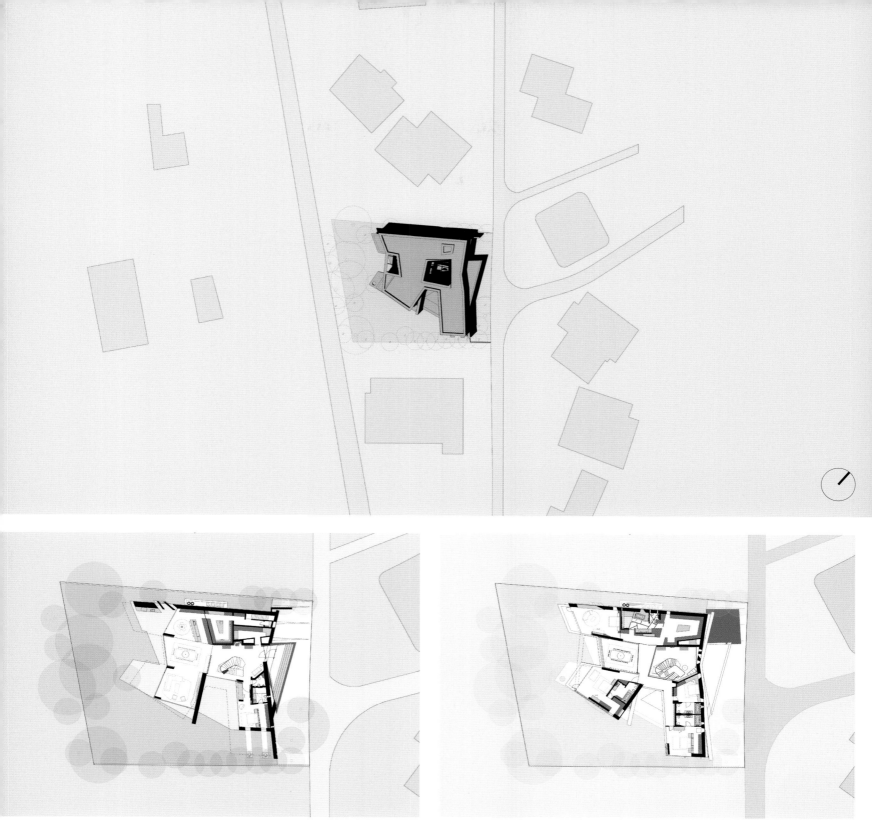

Opposite The cladding refines the appearance of the exterior, which involved huge complexity to maximize insulation, energy efficiency and structural strength, eradicating heat transfer and energy loss while accommodating challenging features such as skylights and windows.

Top Site plan

Above left Ground floor

Above right First floor

0 5 10m

0 10 20 30ft

East elevation

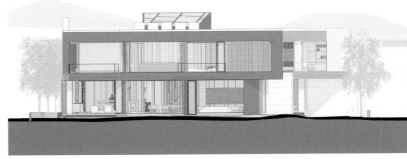

West elevation

Below, clockwise from left Illuminated perforated bronze cladding at entrance · Rheinzink-clad façade in broken bond pattern · High-gloss white lacquer with brass inlays behind the icy white bar · Perforated bronze cladding to entrance façade · Floors and plinth in blackened oak · Large-format Verdi granite tiles · Rheinzink-clad façade

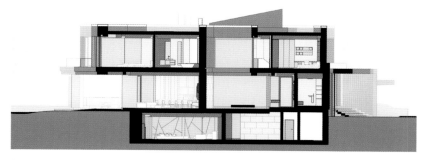
Section

Section

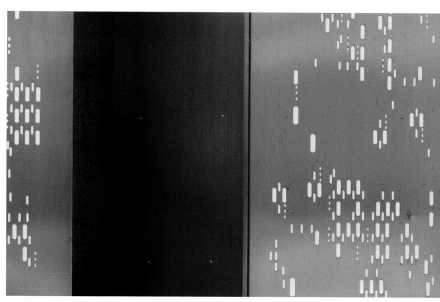

Left A swirling sculptural staircase contrasts playfully with the angular architectural elements where they converge, signalling a subtle change of character between the sociable living space on the ground level and the bedrooms upstairs. The sculpture is *Agata* by Gregory Orekhov.

Opposite top The pinewood that the site overlooks motivates the open, outward-facing orientation of the design, which celebrates the heat of summer but also invites as much natural light in as possible during the dark winter months.

Opposite bottom The shimmering crystal interior has an enchanting, jewel-like quality, with a more whimsical, uplifting, playful quality compared to the exterior. The icy white of the vodka bar echoes the character of the landscape in the winter season.

IKOYI
Lagos   Nigeria

Opposite The penthouse tops an expressive sculptural base of rental apartments and a clubhouse, with a white façade that defines the building's silhouette in the Lagos streetscape.

Following spread The terrace is wrapped with a subtly varied canopy that not only captures the cooling ocean breezes at this height, but also provides privacy among the tall buildings around the apartments while enabling views and easy access to outdoor space and a rim-flow pool.

This double-volume penthouse in Lagos, Nigeria, was commissioned by Reni Folawiyo, founder of ALÁRA, a pioneering West African contemporary design and lifestyle concept store. Reni is renowned as a tastemaker and a champion of contemporary African design.

The architecture of the apartment building, together with the interiors of the penthouse, is a related exploration of local, continental and international design. It is a rooted experiment exploring a path for African modernity in the energetic and rapidly expanding city of Lagos, the heart of Africa's largest economy.

The penthouse tops a crisp white sculptural plinth made up of a series of staggered 'stacked boxes' consisting of apartments. The penthouse is raised above the tree canopy, opening on to a large terrace with a rim-flow pool, wrapped with a semi-permeable shading device that replicates the dappled shade beneath the city's tropical palm trees. The canopy's V-shaped structural supports bring an appropriate sense of scale and interest to the double-volume space.

Arrival at the penthouse follows a staged spatial progression via a separate lobby and lift – with a deliberately compressed sense of space – through a front door set perpendicular to the view, which further de-emphasizes it. This delay heightens the impact of the view when it is finally revealed, an effect that, coupled with the exaggerated expansion of space afforded by a direct visual connection with the horizon, gives the feel of an immersive cinematographic experience.

The interior spaces in the apartment are highly connected, spilling over, through and into each other, lending and borrowing space from one other, blurring the distinction between what is inside and what outside. Simple, restrained natural materials bring softness and warmth to the grand proportions of the apartment. Dark granite floors define the ground plain, pushing the art and furnishings forward.

The interiors, designed with ARRCC, are at once boldly individualistic and a conscious, sustained exploration of contemporary African art and design, particularly as it relates to global luxury. They combine a complex layering of contemporary and vintage pieces, ranging from early 20th-century Moroccan rugs to bespoke articles from Europe and the USA. The emphasis on individual items rather than a predetermined 'scheme' sustains the apartment's sense of evolution and exploration rather than a desire to make a definitive statement.

The cumulative effect of the architecture, interior design and art stands as a watershed in Lagos, embodying its optimistic contemporary African spirit.

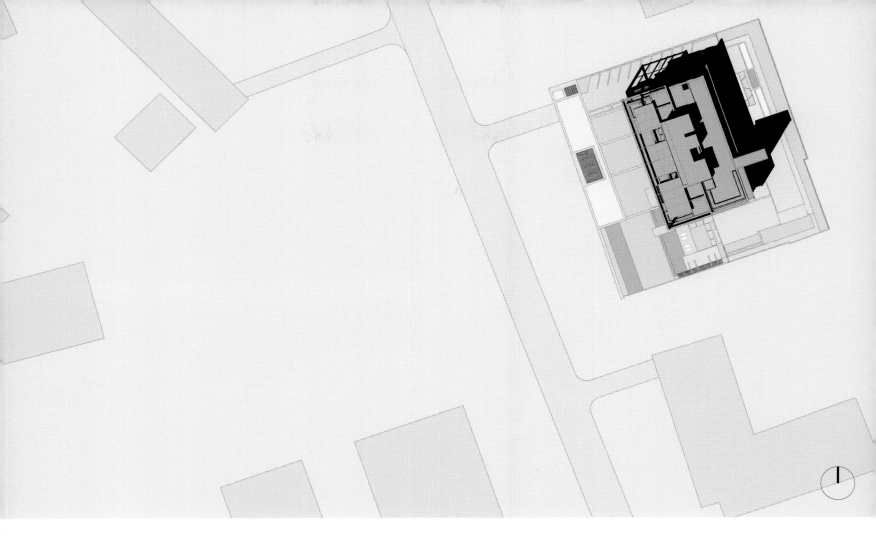

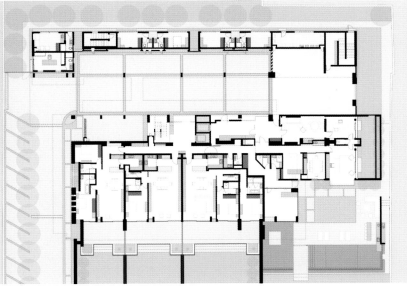

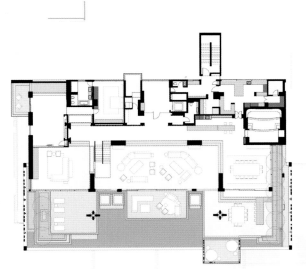

Opposite The canopy rests on V-shaped structural supports, partly inspired by palms. From the rim-flow pool terrace, views of the 'green carpet' of the urban forest canopy roll out beyond.

Top Site plan

Above left Ground floor

Above right Penthouse

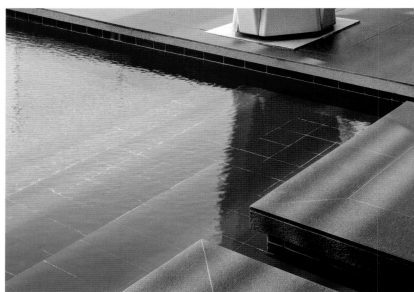

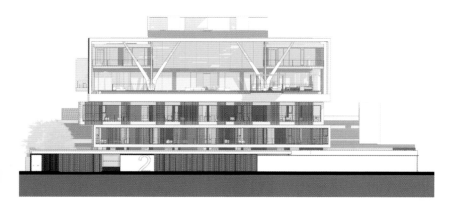

West elevation

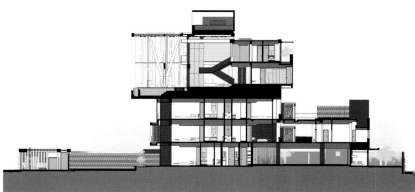

Section

Above, clockwise from left Powder-coated aluminium panels forming the canopy screen • Steel staircase in main living area • Timber cladding throughout the home • A series of staggered 'stacked boxes' • Dark granite floors throughout • The canopy's V-shaped structure • Rim-flow pool on the terrace

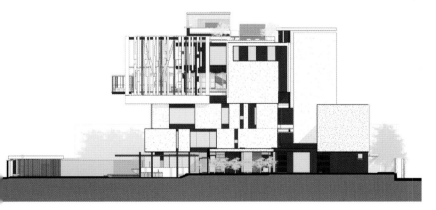

South elevation

Left The timber cladding and dark granite floors are simple and restrained, heightening the impact of the furnishings and art. The artworks are by Nacho Carbonell.

Opposite top The main sitting area combines contemporary and vintage design from Africa, including early 20th-century Moroccan rugs and tapestries, with bespoke pieces from Europe and the USA and creatively repurposed pieces such as the Giant Gear Coffee Table by Jérôme Abel Seguin. The artworks are by Nacho Carbonell and Wim Botha.

Opposite bottom Behind the double-volume living spaces, which open to meet the view over the city, lower volumes in the kitchen (and dining room, visible above), for example, create more intimate spaces on a cosier scale. The artwork is by Wim Botha.

Opposite
While reflecting an exuberance and spontaneity in their bold colour, graphics and geometry, the interiors are a reflection of considered choices guided not merely by taste and whim, but by a sustained understanding of the life-enhancing potential of design. The artwork is by Dominique Zinkpè.

Right The combination of cutting-edge contemporary design and traditional references to African culture has its basis in a refined but experimental approach, curated to be culturally and artistically pioneering. Traditional Fulani poufs and baskets are seen here, while the artwork is by Owusu Ankomah.

Following spread From their raised position above the frenetic pace of the city below, almost like a 'floating villa', the living spaces and terrace provide a sense of calm and release. The living areas below are linked with the bedrooms above via a sculptural black steel-clad staircase. The artworks are by Nacho Carbonell and Wim Botha.

Pages 242–43
View from Table Mountain, Cape Town, South Africa.

COLLABORATION
SAOTA, ARRCC AND OKHA

We are interested in the lived experience of our buildings, in the experience of place rather than in the building just as an architect-designed object. This means that the different disciplines – architecture, interior architecture, interior design and landscaping – are treated as a single process. When architecture seeks to be immersive, when the view of a distant horizon is as integral to an interior as the feel of the flooring underfoot, when the quality of the space is as fundamental as the programme, every detail can contribute to the ultimate effect.

SAOTA's associated studios, ARRCC and OKHA, focusing respectively on interior design and furniture design, grew from this insight.

ARRCC was originally established as Antoni Associates in 1996, nearly a decade after founding director Stefan Antoni launched Stefan Antoni Architects, now SAOTA. A year later, in 1997, OKHA followed. OKHA takes its name from an old Xhosa word for the tradition of carrying fire from house to house through a village in the evening, igniting the hearths and bringing warmth to the interiors and light to the windows. This local tradition evokes both the primal force and the poetic power that interior design and furniture and lighting design have in animating our architecture in a way that is both human and elemental.

While at first each of these three studios might have served to support SAOTA's architectural vision, they have become more established in their own right. All three operate independently, albeit under one roof, and it is common for at least two of them to collaborate on a project; on certain projects, all three work together. The nature of their collaboration has evolved, too, to become a conversation in which each influences the others, impelled by a shared spirit of enquiry that drives innovation in all three studios.

Together, SAOTA, ARRCC and OKHA have worked on projects in eighty-six countries, spanning six continents, with projects in several major cities including Geneva, New York, Dubai, Dakar, Saint-Tropez, and most recently São Paulo and Chengdu.

Perhaps the project that best illustrates the collaboration is Cheetah Plains Game Lodge, led by ARRCC but with meaningful contributions from OKHA and SAOTA.

Cheetah Plains Game Lodge
Situated in the Sabi Sand Game Reserve in eastern South Africa, Cheetah Plains Game Lodge (illustrated on these pages) challenges prevalent ideas about game lodge architecture. Unapologetically architectural, the building is a lens through which visitors experience the environment, its clean, powerful geometry a counterpoint to the organicism of the natural landscape.

The accommodation at Cheetah Plains consists of three independent villas, the Plains Houses, each comprising fragmented clusters of free-standing buildings. This arrangement allows the architecture to accommodate existing natural features such as trees, topography and views, thereby minimizing environmental impact, but also knits the architecture into the landscape, allowing it to become meaningfully integrated with its veld setting.

The clean-lined, angular forms of the lodge buildings consciously play the architecture against its natural setting, creating a tension in the contrast between the seemingly opposing forces of nature and artifice. The expansive cantilevered roof structures and open, seamless boundaries between inside and outside have the effect of immersing guests in the environment. This architectural response facilitates a much more profound and layered interaction with the wilderness and differs vastly from the remote

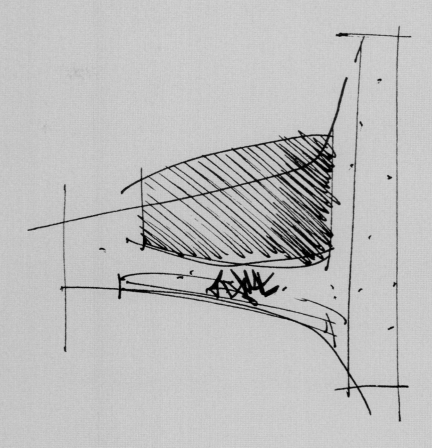

spectatorship from a raised platform typical of lodge design in the colonial tradition.

While the expressed materiality and clean-lined, geometric forms of steel, glass and fair-faced concrete articulate the manufactured qualities of the architecture, the use of raw materials grounds the design in the landscape. Walls built with stone, rusting Cor-Ten steel and timber have been selected to age and weather naturally over time, heightening the connection with the landscape.

The design of the interior adds layers of texture and detail to the architecture, the sensuous use of materials of the furniture contrasting with the grittiness of the rough stone walls, raw concrete and weathered steel. Materials drawn directly from the land are reinterpreted in the interior. Hand-packed mica stone walls dominate, and dining tables made from timber harvested from trees that had fallen naturally in the veld anchor the spaces.

In other furniture pieces specially designed for the project, natural stone, including marble, was selected for its inherent beauty, while metal elements such as mild steel, brass and copper were treated with various oxidization, patination and etching processes to create lustre and depth. Raw natural materials that resonate with the landscape are also treated as if they were precious, transforming them into objects of luxury. Each bar has been hand-carved from a single block of travertine.

At Cheetah Plains, the integrated concept of architecture, interiors and furniture design sustain the vision of the project throughout, considering the design of every element both individually and as part of the greater design and the landscape beyond.

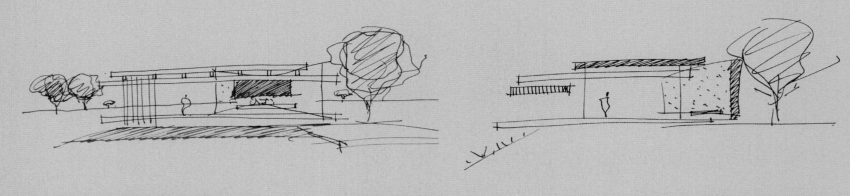

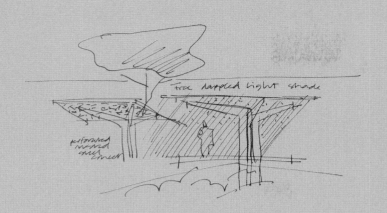

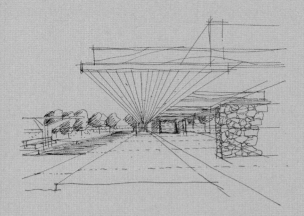

LAKE HOUSE
Lake Geneva   Switzerland

This family home on the banks of Lake Geneva in Switzerland, designed for Senegalese businessman Yerim Sow, draws on the owner's heritage to advance an emerging African-inspired aesthetic in its sculptural form, materiality and textural quality. Perhaps most emphatically, it departs from conventional European typologies in the way it connects with its surroundings.

Strict planning parameters and the restrictive triangular shape of the site prompted the architects to carve architectural forms from the triangular footprint and create a 'reductive' sculptural design of round-edged cubes and triangular masses. The African influence emphasized the roof as the principal sheltering device rather than the wall, prioritizing the indoor–outdoor connection.

The main house is primarily defined by an L-shaped double-volume living area with a curved wall on the façade facing the lake. The living area flows into a dining area and kitchen on the ground floor. The bedrooms, a lobby and en-suite bathrooms occupy the top level. The top floors are accessed by a lift encased in a glass cylinder.

The annexe houses the guest suite. The buildings are linked underground by a cinema, spa, auditorium and garages, which open on to a view down to the lake. Above ground, they are separated by a 20m- (66ft-) wide paved area.

The sloped façade of the main house, clad in aluminium-wrapped composite panels, reflects the triangular shape of the site. Steel and glass predominate, warmed by accents of natural stone and slatted timber on the garage.

The annexe is finished in floor-to-ceiling fixed glazed panels and glazed sliding doors. Timber finishes visually link the two buildings above ground while hinting at their subterranean connection.

The living room is divided into two zones: a formal area and a more informal arrangement centred on the feature fireplace. The irregular shapes of the main living spaces prompted the use of rounded and organic-shaped furnishings. The modern architecture and contemporary interiors are offset with ethnic crafts, including African ceramics. Internally, the main finishes include various types of marble for floors and feature walls, stainless-steel wall cladding, glass, and walnut for joinery finishing.

A whimsical element in the room is the horse lamp from MOOOI, which blurs the boundary between the interior and the exterior by playfully inverting expectations, with its life-size sculpted form on the inside of the glazed façade.

Architect of record: SRA Kössler & Morel Architects

Opposite The roof meets the ground in a pinpoint, drawing the eye to the ground plane and landscape.

The home sits alongside Lake Geneva and is constructed from various building materials including stone, steel, concrete, glass and marble. The veranda space is an extension of the social rooms on the ground floor, encouraging indoor–outdoor living.

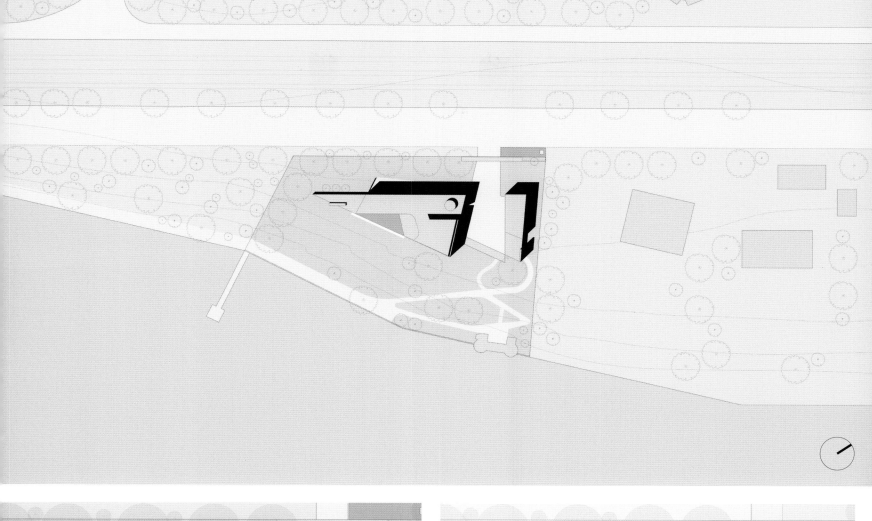

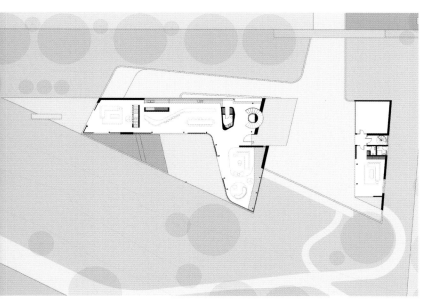

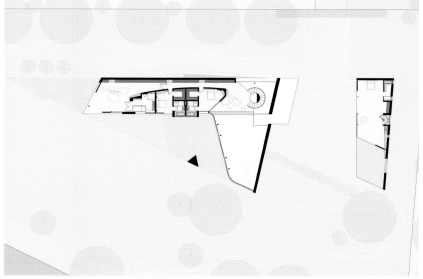

Opposite top The main house is a combination of round-edged cubes and triangular masses that form the L-shape. A curved wall on the façade facing the lake creates an organic character expressed in dark grey Alucobond and glass. Horse Lamp is by MOOOI.

Opposite bottom The living area features marble floors, stainless-steel wall cladding, glass, and walnut for joinery finishing.

Top Site plan

Above left Ground floor

Above right First floor

```
0        5      10m
0    10    20  30ft
```

South-east elevation

Above, clockwise from left Chandore limestone: a play of positive and negative on the building façade • Inclined face of Alucobond and Rheinzink wall cladding • Glass and walnut timber screen • External triangular façade of glass and Rheinzink • Chandore limestone with inset strips of stainless steel • A Carolina Sardi art installation: painted steel oval discs suspended off the panelled wall face • Boulders from site excavation used as natural embankments

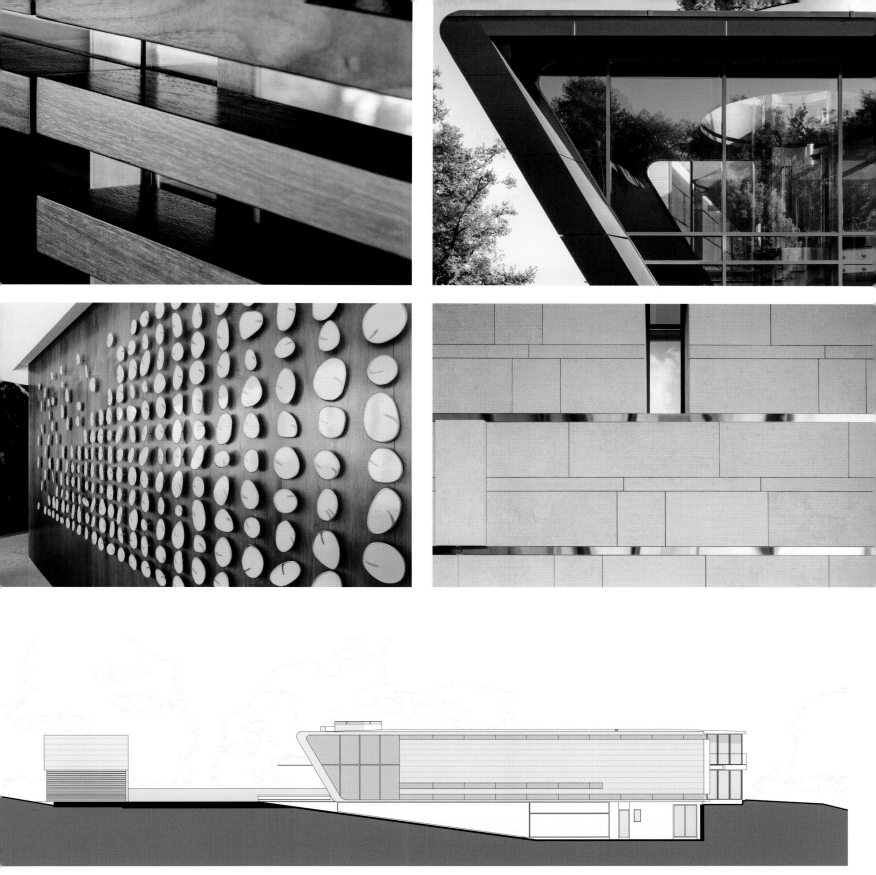

North-west elevation

Left The pool side of the home faces Lake Geneva.

Opposite top The main entrance sits between a sloped façade and a stone-clad wall.

Opposite bottom Conceptually, the home's emphasis on the flat roof rather than the vertical wall, allowing a powerful connection to the surroundings, particularly the view of the lake, has its origins in a distinctively African view of shelter.

COURBE

Lac Leman   Switzerland

Opposite The impact of
the sun is moderated by a
laser-cut aluminium shade
screen that follows the
curves of the roof and plan.

Following spread The curved,
wing-like shape of the front
façade is an architectural
response to the contoured
topography of the site. Seen
from the water, the house
appears almost at one with the
wooded hills that rise gently
out of the lake and, at the
same time, very different from
the traditional suburbia that
surrounds it.

Just as its Alpine setting has been formed by many forces ove
time, Courbe, on Lac Leman in Switzerland, is a residence shaped
intuitively and iteratively by many elements – from sun and topography
to brief and local zoning regulations.

The property is entered from the street, and the design negotiates
the lakeside slope in a series of full-width 'slices' that contour across
the wedge-shaped site. The first of these is a triple-storey light scoop
that houses a gallery space and creates a threshold to the more
private parts of the house. Guests can circulate vertically down to a
top-lit basement art space that opens up into an entertainment area
Functionally separated in the slice closest to the lake, the principal
living rooms are on the ground floor: a sequence of dining, kitchen
and family rooms is sheltered below an upper storey housing the
bedrooms, while a double-height living room noses towards the lake
creating shelter from the cold north wind.

Entry is on a mid-level below a suspended canopy that furthe
parts the slices into two wings and, in doing so, opens up a view
across the lake to the mountains beyond. Swooping down between
these wings, a sculptural planted roof both echoes a distinctive fold
in the distant Alpine skyline and responds to prescriptions in the local
zoning scheme.

Sunlight is the other guiding force that shapes the spaces and forms
The site responds to its north-west orientation, and every effort was
made to bring south light into the house. Carving the programme into
parallel slices exposes two south elevations. The first of these – at the
entrance – is largely closed up with zinc cladding to provide privacy
but high-level clerestory windows scoop art-friendly light deep into the
basement gallery. The fissure between the slices creates a generous
and private south-facing courtyard in the centre of the plan and this
in turn, has a light well cored out into the basement below. The roo
is punctured with skylights, while the pool is also used as a sort o
lightbox, with a glass wall bouncing light into the basement. The resul
is a series of luminous spaces characterized by varying types of ligh

Materials were chosen to respond to these bright spaces. In the
main living spaces, rich timber ceilings and natural stone walls add
warmth and texture. Black marble shot through with white veins, and
limestone layered in horizontal bands, echo snow-clad peaks and
sedimentary rocks, while front door and gates open up in copper-clad
clockwork. Concrete is also used in a variety of ways, from heavy
board-formed panels in the entrance hall, to the monolithic curve o
the pool cabana, to the curtain-like walls of the basement pool and spa

Architect of record: SRA Kössler & Morel Architects

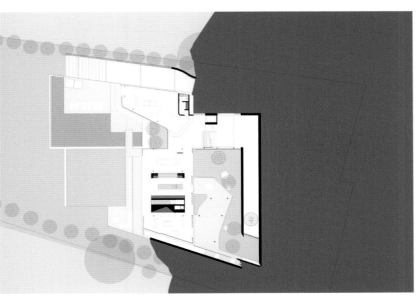

Previous spread Zinc-clad on the outside, the entrance appears robust and opaque. A suspended canopy provides cover at the main entrance, situated between two wings.

Opposite top A private, south-facing courtyard is located in the centre of the plan.

Opposite bottom White walls and ceilings help to bounce and reflect light in the principal living areas: the result is a series of luminous daylit spaces.

Top Site plan

Above left Ground floor

Above right First floor

0   5   10m

0   10   20 30ft

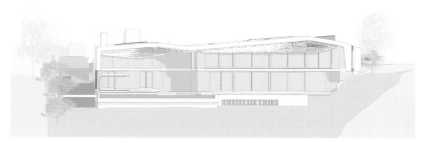

West elevation

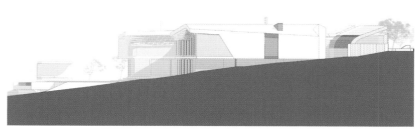

South elevation

Above, clockwise from left Front door that opens up in copper-clad clockwork • Concrete curtain-like walls of the basement pool and spa • Concrete entrance wall • Smoked eucalyptus timber ceiling • Marble staircase panel • Helical staircase in rustic oiled raw steel • Black marble shot through with white veins

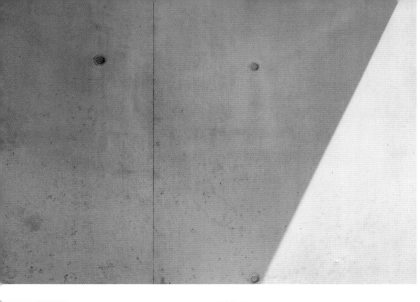

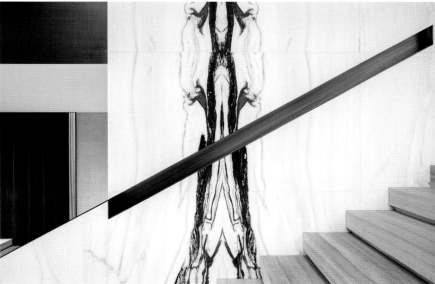

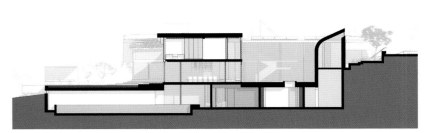

Section

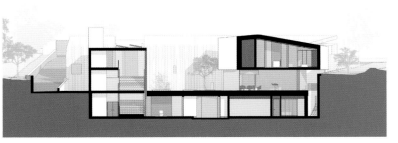

Section

Opposite A view of the lake can be seen through the home from the front door.

Right Soft art-friendly light filters down to the basement gallery, while the basement areas within the deep light scoop are lined with white walls and ceilings.

Following spread In the main living spaces, rich timber ceilings and natural stone walls combine to add warmth and texture. The roof is punctured with strategically placed skylights.

HURON

Ontario   Canada

This summer house is set on the banks of Lake Huron in a small, remote Canadian town about an hour's drive from London, Ontario. While the architectural context might be characterized as somewhat conservative 'cabin country', this house attempts to extend the possibilities of the traditional lakeside family retreat through a contemporary approach, harnessing developments in design, technology and sustainability to connect with its beautiful natural setting while exploring new ways of enhancing the lifestyle experience of the family summer getaway. The architects have taken great care to keep the design unobtrusive and sensitive to its setting, while still making an architectural statement.

The site is a bluff occupying the transitional space between water and forest, rising 3.5m (11ft) from road level and then dropping down to the water to create a grassy embankment. The building is set back on the property towards the street to preserve the natural bluff. The rear of the house, facing Lake Huron, dissolves into a two-storey wall of glass washing natural light deep into the interiors.

Conceptually, the design consists of a series of stacked and suspended rectangular boxes, one embedding the building into the ground plane, the other suspended overhead to allow the living level to exist between the volumes. An indoor–outdoor volume to the south anchors the building and maximizes the site's lakeside views while allowing the living spaces to occupy the foreground. A bank of bedrooms projects backwards above the garage.

The way in which the building is largely obscured from the street and in turn screens views of the lake helps build suspense on arrival, satisfying the sense of anticipation on entry via the large pivot door. From the threshold, a dramatic triple-volume atrium lets in natural light and draws the eye outwards towards the view.

Programmatically, in keeping with the client brief, the spaces are fluid, the levels easy to navigate and the layout simple and well structured, allowing for a casual atmosphere. The vast central volume is subtly contrasted with more intimate and contained volumes in the kitchen and other living spaces for a varied spatial experience.

The upper level housing the main bedroom is devoted entirely to the owners' private space, including an office and a gym. To the front of the house, a covered outdoor entertainment area flanks a swimming pool.

The finishes, externally and internally, favour a ceramic-panelled system robust and hard-wearing enough to endure the extremes of the Canadian climate. The interior decoration was by ARRCC, the interiors division of SAOTA.

Architect of record: Matter Architectural Studio Inc.

Opposite The mass of the monolithic façade, which deliberately obscures the view of the lake at the entrance of the house, is broken down and rendered less imposing by the clever use of contrasting dark and light sections and reflective windows.

Following spread The design consists of two rectangular boxes set at right angles. The living spaces occupy the 'floating' lightbox facing the lake while a dark-coloured bank embedded in the landscape projects backwards, housing the bedrooms, with the garages below.

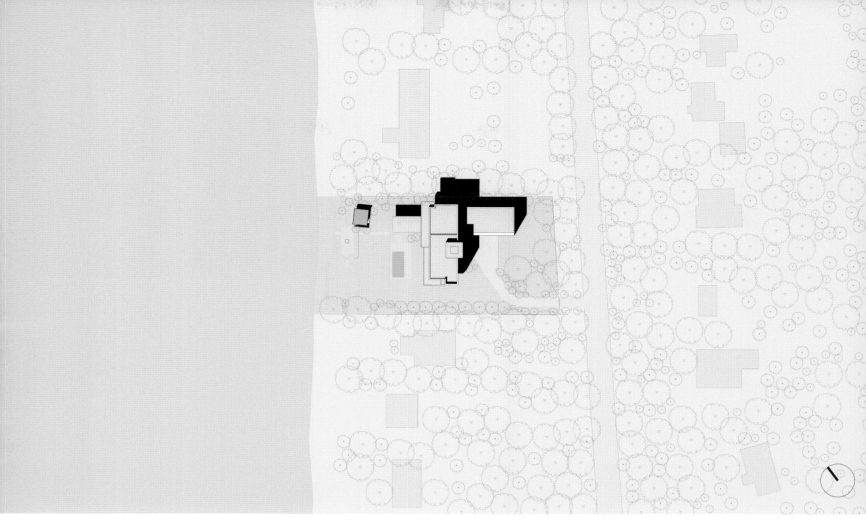

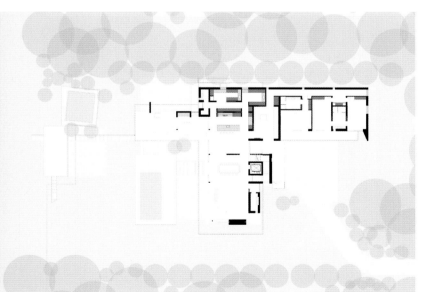

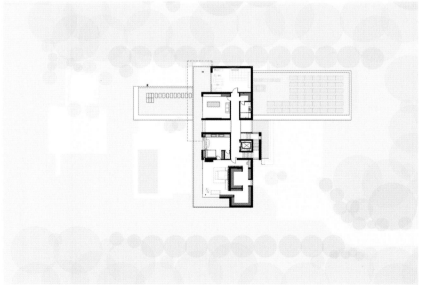

Opposite top In contrast to the street-facing façade, the rear of the house, facing Lake Huron, dissolves into a two-storey wall of glass.

Opposite bottom A boardwalk and staircase descend to a refurbished cabin that predated the house (just visible at left), and now houses a guest suite and additional outdoor entertainment area to facilitate long summer days playing on the lake.

Top Site plan

Above left Ground floor

Above right First floor

0   5   10m
0   10   20 30ft

West elevation

South elevation

Below, clockwise from left Gunmetal-grey front door and grey-washed oak timber • Everest LED pendant lights by Elan Lighting • Kitchen ceiling interior in Neolith Strata Argentum sintered stone • Double-volume grey-washed oak timber screens • Fireplace and feature screen in Neolith Krater sintered stone • Side wall staircase panel in Neolith Nero Zimbabwe sintered stone • Façade in Neolith Strata Argentum sintered stone

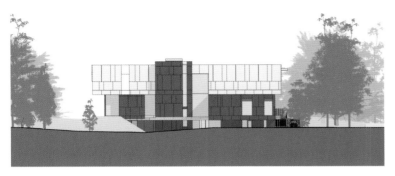

East elevation

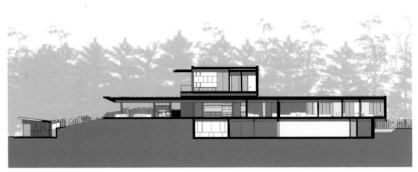

Section

Left External finishes are hard-wearing for the Canadian climatic extremes. The top level is a light, textured finish allowing the pristine floating box to blend with the snowy landscape in winter and the bright sky in summer. The two lower levels are clad in a dark, textured finish to merge with the darker surrounding landscape and forest.

Opposite A triple volume over the sitting area not only allows natural light deep into the living spaces, but also draws the eye outwards towards the view of the lake on an appropriately dramatic scale.

Opposite top The outdoor areas towards the south of the house include a swimming pool and a covered outdoor entertainment area, extending the usable living space into the landscape.

Opposite bottom The light colours of the interiors towards the front of the house emphasize the the height and volumes, while the darker colours towards the back of the living area accentuate the illusion of depth.

Right Strategically placed windows and apertures capture views of surrounding landscape and trees, further integrating interior and exterior and knitting the house into its setting.

STRADELLA

Los Angeles   USA

Stradella, SAOTA's first completed project in Los Angeles, is a remodelled 1970s house on a promontory in Bel Air. The original layout
site and dwelling were planned to ensure privacy from the stre
and to address spectacular views over the city basin. By reinforci
or extending where necessary, generous openings were created
draw in the natural light and rolling vistas.

An attractive approach via a wooded hillside leads to a lea
forecourt, where the arrival façade was reimagined as a sculptu
composition. A massive buttress ties the house into the hillside a
stone-faced walls incised with vertical screens hover over glazing, lea
ing the eye into the house. From the entrance lobby, an asymmetri
passage delays the reveal of the skyline as the weighty forms of t
entrance give way to a lighter structure that floats above the view

The porous nature of the reconfigured floorplan pays homa
to the utopian California modernism of the groundbreaking Ca
Study Houses (1945–66) with light, fresh and open internal spac
that connect the various functions necessary for modern family livi
and grand entertaining. Where possible, walls were replaced by fu
height glazing with sliding windows pocketing or stacking to crea
generous openings. Key bedrooms and bathrooms were redesign
to spill out on to external terraces.

The front terrace was reconfigured to include a new pool. A 40
(131ft-) long linear canopy amplifies the width of the site, extendi
internal living spaces, improving the flow and providing comfortab
outdoor spaces. This canopy – reminiscent of Pierre Koenig's Sta
House (1960; Case Study House #22) – floats over the east terra
lending coherence to the remodelled elements of the dwelling a
to a new theatre and dining wing on the north of the site. It bridg
the original exit driveway and defines a new motor court, where
gym and spa, cellar and staff spaces are accommodated at baseme
level, allowing the ground floor to remain open.

The palette balances warm, natural tones against the bold mass
and crisp linear forms of the architecture. French limestone a
white plaster walls are enlivened inside and out by bronze anodize
aluminium screens and light-grey window frames.

Planted spaces soften the architectural forms and allow a mo
intimate experience of the leafy site. Existing twin palms were retain
at the pool terrace and low-level planting and lawn ensures functio
outdoor spaces and uncluttered views.

Architect of record: PECK Architecture

Opposite A generous
new linear canopy hovers
effortlessly over the terrace,
creating natural extensions
of internal living spaces
and framing twin palms
carefully retained from the
existing landscaping.

Following spread The
arrival court presents
weighty sculptural forms and
screened glazing above a
transparent entrance, which
teasingly draws the eye in and
through the lobby towards
the view, while intentionally
delaying the reveal of the
downtown skyline.

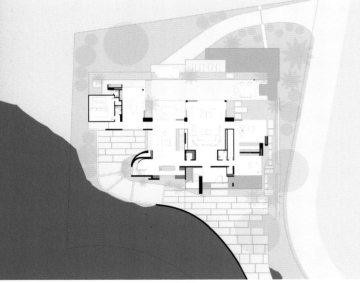

Opposite top The dining room incorporates full-height glazing with sliding doors to create expansive openings.

Opposite bottom The main living spaces on the ground floor are light and open with uncluttered views of the horizon.

Top Site plan

Above left Ground floor

Above right First floor

0   10   20m

0   20   40   60ft

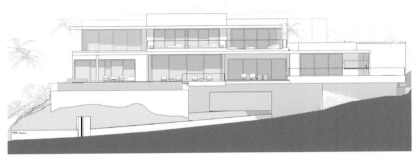

East elevation

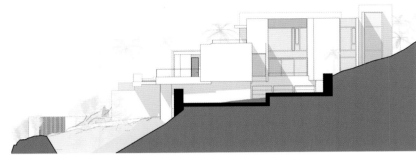

North elevation

Below, clockwise from left Linear canopy framing the sky and palm trees · Linear canopy · Silver travertine used for the bathroom · Anodized-aluminium screens · French limestone · Ashwood with bronze anodized-aluminium screen · Bronze anodized-aluminium staircase balustrade screen

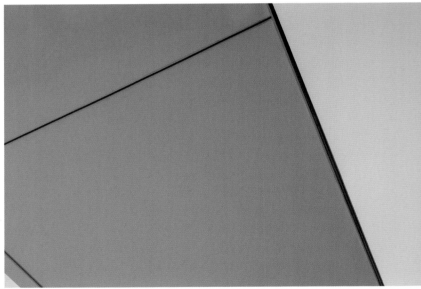

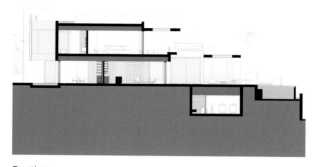

Section

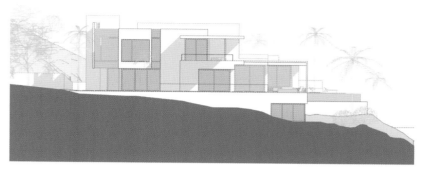

South elevation

Left The linear canopy floats over the east terrace, drawing a frame around the sky and palm trees.

Opposite The study, which looks out over a water feature to the planted forecourt, features light-grey window frames and full-height windows that slide away completely.

Following spread In the forecourt, additional planting enhanced the tree-lined driveway, while a mature tree was retained as a feature.

HILLSIDE
Los Angeles   USA

SAOTA's Hillside home in Los Angeles is located immediately above Sunset Boulevard on a promontory just one over from Pierre Koenig's landmark Stahl House of 1960. The site is a 1,860sq m (20,000sq ft) estate, featuring 300-degree views over the LA skyline and the city basin below, and the design was conceived of more as a self-contained oasis than a conventional house.

The Stahl House served as a key point of departure. The forms and articulation of Hillside's roof planes, which were pushed as far forward as possible so that they could create meaningful external covered living spaces, set its architecture in dialogue with the iconic silhouette nearby and connect it to the drama of its context.

The projecting eaves and soffits create a 'fifth' façade and proved fortuitous in creating a sense of identity, because the wraparound perimeter views necessitated the carefully controlled placement of solid walls and extensive use of glass to maximize the panoramic potential of the site. Consequently the architecture is defined through the floating, overlapping horizontal floor and roof plates curating specific view axes rather than mass walls or external structure.

The steep approach from below resulted in a dramatic entrance through a top-lit central atrium, rising via an underground garage and an indoor waterfall, before surfacing into the centre of the living level in a dramatic moment of revelation as a view of downtown LA opens up. The programme is arranged around this focal view, loosely forming two wings, one oriented east–west and the other north–south. The open-plan interior, in the absence of mass walls, has been articulated vertically and through volumetric changes to rationalize the layout.

References to modernist construction techniques are picked up in the articulation of the steel columns and the sensuous and tactile use of timber and limestone on the floors and walls. Some of the identifying features such as the cut-outs in the roof have been reprised in the detailing of the interior ceilings to add interest.

SAOTA conceived of the programme as a series of living rooms connected to extensive covered outdoor terraces. These are in turn enclosed by a vast undulating rim-flow pool and lush landscaping along the perimeter, subtly screening neighbouring properties with climbing ficus trees.

In keeping with the principles taken from the Stahl House and the pioneering Los Angeles Case Study Houses, built between 1945 and 1966, the generous allocation of outdoor space maximizes the potential of the liveable climate, reconnecting contemporary LA architecture with a somewhat lost aspect of its modernist heritage.

Architect of record: Woods + Dangaran

Opposite Ascending from Sunset Boulevard, the first impression of the building is from below, where the bold forms and material treatments of the eaves and soffits pay homage to the distinctive silhouette of Pierre Koenig's landmark Stahl House nearby.

Following spread The living rooms are connected to extensive covered outdoor terraces bordered by an undulating rim-flow pool set in lush landscaping. Custom outdoor furniture is by Exteta.

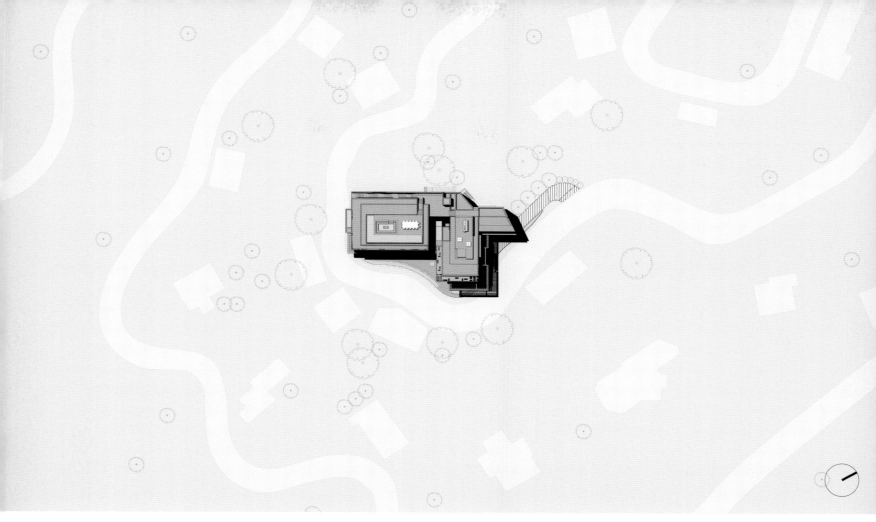

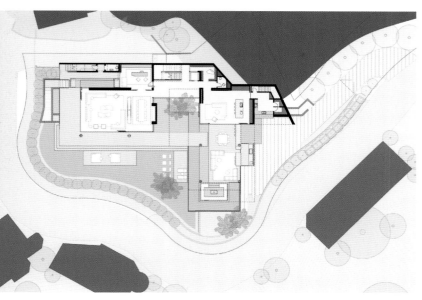

Opposite top A vast rim-flow pool snakes around the exterior of the house and the poolside terraces with panoramic views of the city basin and skyline beyond, giving the property the feel of a retreat in the sky rather than a conventional house.

Opposite bottom Tactile use of timber and French limestone in the main bedroom is also carried extensively throughout the interior and exterior detailing. The artwork on the far wall is *nordiska fondkommissionen "old town depot cafe" "boulder city nevada"/onsale.com* by Petra Cortright.

Top Site plan

Above left First floor

Above right Second floor

Section

East elevation

Below, clockwise from left Entrance door in blackened steel with black patina • Chemical-treated brass entrance gate • Gris du Marais marble kitchen island • Entrance wall with vertical wall garden • Pool deck in Esthec Terrace Emotion with cobalt-blue mosaic tiles • Gris du Marais marble kitchen island • Feature ceiling in Thermory wood

8408 HILLSIDE AVE

North elevation

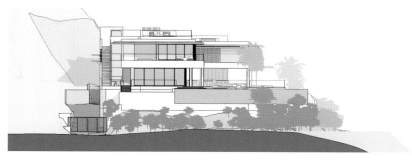

South elevation

Left The horizontal emphasis of the floating, overlapping floor and roof plates, grounded with the use of natural tactile materials such as the timber screens in the exterior detailing, is something of a departure from typical LA modernist architecture.

Opposite The blackened-steel front door opens to a custom-made bar by Henge in the entrance. The artwork is *Dependent* by Yaw Owusu.

Left A staircase takes visitors from the twelve-car garage at basement level, which is itself designed as indoor entertainment space, up to the main living areas. The artwork is *Red Americana* by Kour Pour.

Opposite The house has key outdoor entertainment areas, facilitating an indoor–outdoor lifestyle connected with the setting.

TIMELINE

Stefan Antoni opens first studio
The studio begins life in April 1986, when architect Stefan Antoni, then a young graduate from the University of Cape Town's School of Architecture, starts on his own from his apartment–office in London Road, Sea Point.

Second office Moves to the second office at 34 Loop Street, a three-storey Victorian building.

Third office In 1992 the firm expands and moves to a bigger studio in Church Street. The ceilings are removed to expose the timber beams, resulting in more than ten truckloads of sawdust needing to be taken away. The space is an oven in the summer and a fridge in the winter. The following winter we install insulation, which helps.

Greg Truen joins Stefan Antoni Architects.

Fire! In Church Street office roof

Firemen douse city centre roof blaze

1986	**1995**

Fireman's Arms   Cape Town, South Africa

LGV   Cape Town, South Africa

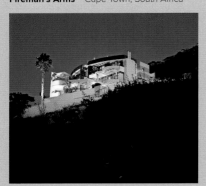

Sachs   Cape Town, South Africa

In 1986 Stefan completes his first non-residential project – the Fire Escape – an addition to the legendary Fireman's Arms, one of Cape Town's oldest establishments, dating back to 1864. Ironically, the morning of its opening, the building inspector condemns the building for not having a fire escape. A hasty arrangement is concluded with a neighbouring property, allowing access over their land. This out-of-the-box thinking will become a hallmark of the firm's work.

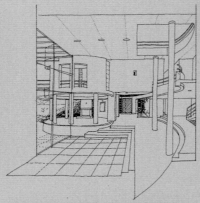

Cunningham   Cape Town, South Africa

Throughout the early 1990s, various Atlantic Seaboard houses are designed and completed by Stefan Antoni Architects. The office flourishes. In 1997 it is decided to build the fourth office at 186 Loop Street, with a penthouse for Greg on the roof.

Emmanuels   Cape Town, South Africa

Calabrese   Cape Town, South Africa

House Santer   Cape Town, South Africa
SAIA (South African Institute of Architects) Award

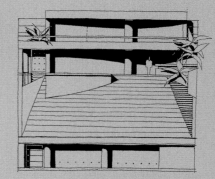

Philip Olmesdahl joins Stefan Antoni Architects.

The three seniors Haydn Ellis, Greg Truen and Stefan Antoni at house LGV

ARRCC starts as Antoni Associates.

Fourth office

Mark Rielly joins Stefan Antoni Architects.

OKHA founded At the time, there are only three well-known furniture suppliers in Cape Town. We open a store, OKHA, an old Xhosa word to describe bringing fire from house to house in the evenings — most apt, an interior decor firm lighting up people's homes.

Flood! Towards the end of our stay in our fourth office, the new owner of the roof space removes waterproofing midwinter — the office floods for weeks.

O K H A

1996

1998

Tamkar Cape Town, South Africa

Imara Marbella, Spain

In the late 1990s we are approached by a German developer living in Marbella, Spain, to design a housing estate called Imara. Planning hurdles delay the project for more than five years, but eventually permission is granted to commence. It is designed in the local pueblo style with a modern twist and sells out prior to completion.

Balducci Restaurant Cape Town, South Africa
PG Bison – Interior Design Excellence Award

Contursi Cape Town, South Africa
SAIA Special Mention

Sprecher Cape Town, South Africa

Baci Cape Town, South Africa
Cavendish Awards – Best Designed Shop

New directors
Greg Truen and Philip Olmesdahl are appointed as directors of Stefan Antoni Architects.

Mark Rielly is appointed as director of Antoni Associates.

Hatfield Church
We purchase an old church at 109 Hatfield Street, which is then converted into what is today the studio's headquarters, Hatfield 109. The new building's façade has mutated many times over the years and serves as a canvas for various artists to showcase their work.

1999

2004

Melkbos   Cape Town, South Africa

Medburn   Cape Town, South Africa

St Leon   Cape Town, South Africa
The extensive cantilevered terraces and roof give St Leon a quality of lightness and elegance.

Alex Junction is a taxi rank and holding facility for 1,000 taxis sitting over a 15,000sq m (161,000sq ft) shopping centre.

Fisherman's 19   Cape Town, South Africa
CIfA & SAIA Awards
Fisherman's 19 becomes our third project to receive an award from the South African Institute of Architects.

Alex Junction   Johannesburg, South Africa
Retail Design Development Awards – Finalist

Cove 6   Knysna, South Africa
Built on a cliff edge overlooking The Cove at Pezula in Knysna, this home was unfortunately destroyed in the Knysna fires of 2017.

Nettleton Pentagon   Cape Town, South Africa

Eventide   Cape Town, South Africa
This nine-storey multi-residential building is built into the cliffside at the edge of Clifton Beach.

Mankgaile Primary School   Limpopo, South Africa
CIfA & SAIA Awards

Hatfield 109
CIfA (Cape Institute for
Architecture) & SAIA Awards

With the global market crash,
local work in South Africa
virtually dries up. SAOTA shifts
focus to global expansion.

**Stefan Antoni Architects
officially becomes Stefan Antoni
Olmesdahl Truen Architects**

**SAOTA joins the architectural
football league**
The studio starts an architectural
football team in the spirit of South
Africa's hosting the 2010 soccer
World Cup.
Currently five-time champions.

Adam Letch
joins the
SAOTA family
as architectural
photographer.

2005

2010

Palm Jumeirah   Dubai, UAE
Our first project in Dubai is located
on one of the most prestigious
tip lots of the Palm Jumeirah, with
views back towards the iconic
downtown and marina of Dubai.

Roca Llisa   Ibiza, Spain
A collaborative project
with ARRCC on the island
of Ibiza.

Victoria   Cape Town, South Africa

Zilwa   Sainte Anne Island, Seychelles

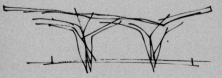

Dakar Towers   Dakar, Senegal
MIPIM Award

Radisson Blu is our first hotel
in West Africa – a 182-room,
five-star hotel situated on the
Corniche in Dakar.

Dubrovnik, Croatia – Libera
Invited Competition. SAOTA
wins an invited competition
against, among others, Zaha
Hadid and Peter Marino.

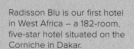

Radisson Blu   Dakar, Senegal

Dubrovnik, Croatia
Libera Invited Competition –
Winner

First international media coverage Lake House is published by The Cool Hunter. Soon afterwards we see a spike in global media coverage, which leads to additional projects abroad.

Stefan Antoni Olmesdahl Truen Architects becomes SAOTA The studio sees rapid growth, especially internationally. We decide to rebrand to SAOTA to stay relevant and to reposition as a global brand.

New directors Jon Case and Michele Rhoda are appointed as directors of ARRCC.

New director Adam Court is appointed as director of OKHA.

SAOTA

2011　　　　　　　　　　　　　　　　　　　　　　**2013**

Colina　Colina, Portugal

Saint-Tropez　Saint-Tropez, France

MTN Headquarters　Abidjan, Ivory Coast

SAOTA sees an expansion not only in the global market, entering new locations, but also in project types, with more commercial commissions.

Boma House　Cape Town, South Africa

Kingsway Tower in Lagos, Nigeria, is a landmark mixed-use building set on a prominent corner on Alfred Rewane Road, an arterial road that bisects the city, leading north towards the airport and south to Victoria Island. The design introduces new architectural ideas to Lagos.

Kingsway Tower　Lagos, Nigeria

Voëlklip　Hermanus, South Africa
SAIA Award

Waterberry　Harare, Zimbabwe

Bellagio　Los Angeles, USA

Virtual reality (VR)
is introduced
to the office.

Ocean View, Africa's record-selling home, is sold for $22 million

30th anniversary celebrations
The office together with ARRCC & OKHA

New directors
Phillippe Fouché and Mark Bullivant are appointed as directors of SAOTA.

New director
Logen Gordon is appointed as director of SAOTA.

After the success of winning the Archititzer A+Popular Choice Awards, Ocean View sells for a record price of $22m — the highest price paid for a house in Africa at the time.

2014

2016

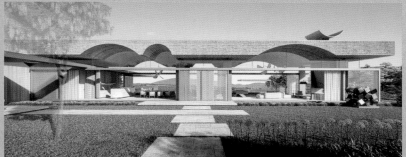

Waterbridge   São Paulo, Brazil

NEB (New Engineering Building), University of Cape Town   South Africa
SAPOA Property Development Awards for Innovative Excellence.

Downtown   Dubai, UAE

Le Pine   Saint-Tropez, France

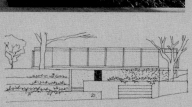
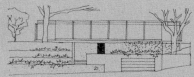

Clifton Terraces is located in the heart of Clifton, Cape Town. The development consists of fourteen apartments.

House Invermark was purchased by SAOTA director Stefan Antoni and care was taken to return the building structure back to its original state, while accentuating existing features and delicately adding additional aspects to enhance the overall composition.

House Invermark   Cape Town, South Africa
ClfA & SAIA Awards (sketch above left)

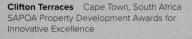

Clifton Terraces   Cape Town, South Africa
SAPOA Property Development Awards for Innovative Excellence

Accra Link   Accra, Ghana

Sultanpur   Sultanpur, India

LIGHT SPACE LIFE

07 DECEMBER 2017
to 02 MARCH 2018

THE ARCHITECT pop up gallery
Cape Institute for Architecture
71 Hout Street, Cape Town CBD

Past, Present & Future Work
SAOTA

LIGHT SPACE LIFE at CIfA, Cape Town
Our first architectural exhibition,
a showcase of past, present and
future work, explores our core values —
Light, Space and Life.

Miami home sells for $22.5 million
SAOTA's first completed project, Pine
Tree in Miami, is sold for $22.5m, the
highest price paid for a single family
home in Miami at the time.

We reach 100k on Instagram

2017   **2019**

The Ritz-Carlton Residences   Bodrum, Turkey

The Ritz-Carlton Residences
in Bodrum mark the first stand-
alone branded residences for
Marriott International in the
Europe, Middle East and
Africa regions.

Oculus is a boutique hotel
coupled with premium
penthouse suites on the water's
edge in Stockholm.

Kacyiru   Kigali, Rwanda

City Heights   Cape Town, South Africa

Glyfada   Athens, Greece

Oculus   Stockholm, Sweden

The Waves   Lagos, Nigeria

Neuländer Quarree   Hamburg, Germany
WAF Award

SAOTA's concept design
for a mixed-use development
in Hamburg, Germany,
receives Highly Commended
in the Residential Future
Project Category at the World
Architecture Festival (WAF).

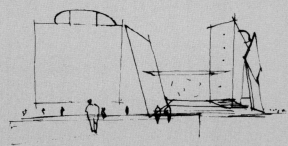

Sales Centre   Chongqing, China

Focus   Dakar, Senegal

New canteen

Launch of Tenebris Lab
The SAOTA-supported VR company propels the firm to the forefront of tech-led architecture and design.

LIGHT SPACE LIFE at Property One in Zurich
Our architectural exhibition opens in Switzerland.

SAOTA-designed Netflix *Selling Sunset* home sells for $35.5 million

COVID-19 WFH We successfully migrate the entire studio to a fully operational working-from-home model.

2020   2021

Kirsch Pharma Health Care   Wedemark, Germany

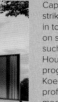

Bel Air 948   Los Angeles, USA

Cape Town and Los Angeles bear striking resemblances to each other in topography and climate and draw on similar architectural movements, such as the post-war Case Study House Program in California. The programme, which saw Pierre Koenig as a key participant, had a profound effect on the design of the modern house in South Africa.

The studio has worked on projects spanning 86 countries, over six continents, with projects currently under way in several major cities, including Geneva, New York, Dubai, Dakar, Saint-Tropez, São Paulo and Shenzhen.

Zinc Tower   Instanbul, Turkey

Cave Tower   Mývatn, Iceland
A competition design for an observation tower in Iceland. The tower acts as a landmark and visitors centre at the Grjótagjá cave, which sits within a fissure created by the American and Eurasian tectonic plates.

Grey Collection   France

La Dôle   Nyon, Switzerland

Bel Air 783   Los Angeles, USA

Bio-Marine Tower   Dubai, UAE

Meguro   Tokyo, Japan

Residential Apartments   Dakar, Senegal

House California   Los Angeles, USA

CREDITS

Over the past few years we have collaborated with incredible designers and consultants, whose contribution has been invaluable to the realization of so many exciting projects. Thank you to those who have contributed, who might not be included below.

ARCHITECTS OF RECORD

H+H Architecture
RyS Arquitectos
KKAID
DVICE INC.
TKD Architects
Cachez Turnkey Projects
SRA Kössler & Morel Architects
Matter Architectural Studio Inc.
PECK Architecture
Woods + Dangaran

INTERIOR DESIGNERS

Studio Parkington
ARRCC
OKHA
Cecile & Boyd
Molteni & C
Lynda Murray Interior Design
Rosy Levy
Max Kasymov
Reni Folawiyo
Thierry Lemaire
MASS Beverly
Minotti Los Angeles

ENGINEERS

Moroff & Kühne Consulting Engineers
JG Afrika
De Villiers & Moore
Saka Undagi Design
Wija Kusuma Nadi

Sutherland Engineers
PLF Structural Engineers
F.G. Engineers, Inc.
GGB Engineering, Inc.
ACOR Consultants
Alexander Boenich
Morgan Omonitan & Abe Ltd
KOA Consultants Ltd
T Ingénierie
E.G.C. Chuard Ingénieurs Conseils SA
BIFF SA – Bureau d'Ingénieur Fenêtres et Façades
Concentric Engineering
Capson Electrical Contractors Ltd
JLA Structural Engineers
Optimus Structural Design
Wsg Engineering

CONTRACTORS

Gossow & Harding Construction Pty (Ltd)
Cape Island Construction
Adi Jaya Utama
Brodson Construction
Woolems, Inc.
Horizon
Alexander Stroikov
Monterosa Construction Ltd
MCI Design-Build Corporation
Gordon Gibson Construction
Fortis Development

LIGHTING DESIGNERS

MADEstudio by Martin Doller Design
Professional Illumination Design
Nipek
Lux Populi
FPOV
Ksenia Rudkovskaya
Oculus Light Studio

LANDSCAPE DESIGNERS

Franchesca Watson Garden Designer

Nicholas Whitehorn Landscape Design

Bali Landscape Company

Cracknell

OVP Associates & AfriServ

Raymond Jungles, Inc.

CLAD Landscape Architecture & Design

Wyer & Co

Klukva Landscaping

Martin Paysage

MHLA Inc.

Fiore Landscape Design

Chris Sosa Landscape Architect

QUANTITY SURVEYORS

SBDS Quantity Surveyors

Penjor Bali Mandiri

Alexander Stroikov

Cachez Turnkey Projects

Meyer Summersgill

PHOTOGRAPHERS

Sergey Ananiev 218, 220–27, © Sergey Ananiev

Karl Beath 140–51, © Karl Beath

Karl Beath and Wieland Gleich 72, 74–9, © Karl Beath
and Wieland Gleich

Myles Beeson 185, © ICON Aircraft

Enda Cavanagh 90, 94 t, 97 tr, © Enda Cavanagh

Greg Cox – Bureaux 129, © Bureaux, 316 City Heights,
© Greg Cox

Nicolas Cuquel for NCWest Production 169 ml, ©
NCWest Production

Dan Forer 316 Miami home, © Dan Forer

Adam Letch 6, 9–22, 24–36, 38–40, 44,
45 t, 46–7, 52 t, 55 tl, mr & bl, 56–7, 60–71, 96 l &
br, 97 bl & br, 99–102, 104–16, 118–28, 130–39, 152,
154–63, 172, 174–84, 186–217, 228, 230–41, 244–50,
256 l & tr, 257, 260, 262–309, 311 Balducci, 312

Nettleton, 314 Kingsway, 315 Ocean View,
Le Pine, NEB, Clifton, Invermark, 317 Kirsch
Pharma, © SAOTA

The Lex Ash 7, © The Lex Ash

Vauban Radi 170 bl & br, 313 mr © Vauban Radi

SAOTA 2–3, 17, 23, 28–9, 37, 43, 45 b, 48–51,
52 b, 55 tr, ml & br, 58–9, 73, 80–81, 91–3,
94 b, 96 tr, 97 tl, 98, 117, 153, 164–65, 166–7,
169 br, 173, 219, 229, 242–43, 251–54, 265
br, 258–59, 261, 310–11 all except Balducci,
312–13 all except Nettleton, Alex Jct, Rocca
Llisa & Radisson Blu, 314–15 Voëlklip, St-
Tropez & all b&w except Ocean View, 316–17
all b&w except Miami home, © SAOTA

Guido Schwarz 312 Mark Rielly, 314 Jon Case,
Michele Rhoda © Guido Schwarz

Lorenzo Vecchia 169 bm, 313 Rocca Llisa tm ©
Lorenzo Vecchia

Steven Wilcox – Unsplash 103, © Steven Wilcox

Elsa Young 312 Alex Junction © Elsa Young

OTHER COLLABORATORS

Graham Wood – Copywriter

JNA Thatchers

Penjor Bali Mandiri – Project Managers

Troy Advisory LLP – Project Managers

Park Lane Projects – Project Managers

Twotimesmono – AV Consultant

Xssentials – AV Consultant

Prime Group Management, LLC
– Owner Representative

Plus Development Group
– Development Managers

Creative Art Partners – Artwork

The Oppenheim Group – Property Agents

Bond Street Partners – Property Agents,
Brokering Company

On the cover: The pool terrace at Ocean View, Cape Town, South Africa.
Image by Adam Letch.

First published in the United Kingdom in 2021 by
Thames & Hudson Ltd, 181A High Holborn, London WC1V 7QX

First published in the United States of America in 2021 by
Thames & Hudson Inc., 500 Fifth Avenue, New York, New York 10110

Light Space Life: Houses by SAOTA © 2021 Thames & Hudson Ltd, London

Text © 2021 SAOTA (Pty) Ltd, Cape Town

Foreword by Reni Folawiyo
"The South African House" by Nic Coetzer
"Patrons" by Stefan Antoni

For image copyright information, please see page 319.

British Library Cataloguing-in-Publication Data
A catalogue record for this book is available from the British Library

Library of Congress Control Number 2021934214

ISBN 978-0-500-34377-7

Printed and bound in China by RR Donnelley

MIX
Paper from
responsible sources
FSC® C144853

Be the first to know about our new releases,
exclusive content and author events by visiting
thamesandhudson.com
thamesandhudsonusa.com
thamesandhudson.com.au